# Teaching with Love

# Rethinking Childhood

Joe L. Kincheloe and Jan Jipson
*General Editors*

Vol. 1

PETER LANG
New York • Washington, D.C./Baltimore
Bern • Frankfurt am Main • Berlin • Vienna • Paris

LISA S. GOLDSTEIN

# Teaching with Love

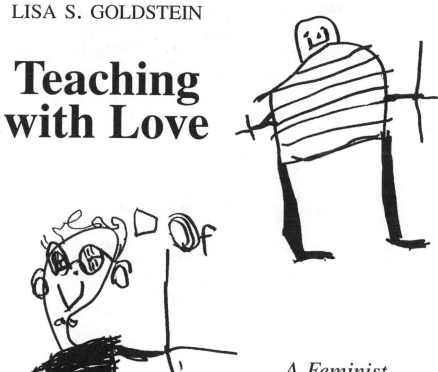

*A Feminist*
*Approach*
*to Early*
*Childhood*
*Education*

PETER LANG
New York • Washington, D.C./Baltimore
Bern • Frankfurt am Main • Berlin •Vienna • Paris

**Library of Congress Cataloging-in-Publication Data**

Goldstein, Lisa S.
Teaching with love: a feminist approach to early childhood education / Lisa S. Goldstein.
p. cm. — (Rethinking childhood; v. 1)
Includes bibliographical references and index.
1. Early childhood education—California—Case studies. 2. Feminism and education—
California—Case studies. 3. Early childhood education—United States. 4. Feminism
and education—United States. I. Title. II. Series.
LB1139.25.G65   372.21—DC20   96-36581
ISBN 0-8204-3481-7
ISSN 1086-7155


**Die Deutsche Bibliothek-CIP-Einheitsaufnahme**

Goldstein, Lisa S.:
Teaching with love: a feminist approach to early childhood education / Lisa S. Goldstein.
–New York; Washington, D.C./Baltimore; Bern; Frankfurt am Main;
Berlin; Vienna; Paris: Lang.
(Rethinking childhood; Vol. 1)
ISBN 0-8204-3481-7
NE: GT

Cover design by James F. Brisson.
Front cover art by Madeline Levinson.
Author photo on back cover by Laura Bottorff.
Interior art by Sam Goldstein.

The paper in this book meets the guidelines for permanence and durability
of the Committee on Production Guidelines for Book Longevity
of the Council of Library Resources.

Printed in the United States of America.

Dedicated
with love, of course
to
Rich, Sam, and Noah

# Acknowledgments

One strategy often suggested to people facing a seemingly impossible challenge is visualization. They are encouraged to visualize themselves succeeding: visualize yourself thin, visualize yourself cancer-free, visualize yourself at the top of Mount Everest, visualize yourself holding your newborn baby. When I began writing this book, I often visualized myself writing these acknowledgments: I knew it would be the last step of the process. I felt as if I'd never get there.

In the end, of course, I did. But it took the support, cooperation, and assistance of a lot of people from all corners of my life. Like a movie star who holds up her Oscar and talks about how it "really belongs" to all of her behind-the-scenes helpers, I'd like to mention all of the people to whom this book really belongs.

First of all, there is the real woman depicted here as "Martha George." For truly, without her I would have no book. She welcomed me into her classroom, gave unstintingly of her time, expertise, and insights, and rode with me on the rollercoaster ride this process became. The book surely belongs to her. Thanks are also due to her principal, "Alexander Ganz," and to all in the administration of the "Loma Prieta Unified School District" for allowing me to do my research at "Bayview School."

This book also belongs to Nel Noddings, who met me as one-caring every step of this journey. She is a shining star in my universe, a model of balancing devoted mothering with devoted scholarship. My gratitude also goes out to Jan Jipson, Lee Shulman, and Stuart Reifel, whose insights and encouragement always came at just the right time; to Debra Freedman for her careful critical reading; and to my resident computer wizard, Rich Goldstein. I would also like to thank Chris Myers and Jackie Pavlovic at Peter Lang for their aid and assistance.

Without the support of a number of outstanding early childhood professionals I would not have been able to write this book. Thanks to the devoted teachers at Stanford Arboretum Children's Center, Sojourner Truth Child Development Center, and Habibi's Hutch Preschool, who took such good care of my boys during the course of this study and during the writing and revisions that followed. I learned a great deal about love's role in the education of young children from these teachers.

I offer a piece of this book to the children I have taught, both in Martha's class and in my own classrooms. I cannot name them here, for reasons of confidentiality, but they have been in my heart every step of the way. I'd like to give special notice to my talented illustrators: Madeline Levinson, Laura Bottorff, and Sam Goldstein.

I also offer a piece of this book to all the friends and family members who put up with unreturned telephone calls, late or forgotten birthday cards, and the constant craziness of my writing frenzy. Extra special thanks go out to the Mountjoys, the Grotes, the Tatums, the Suyemoto/Champagnes, and the Wurtzes.

I would also like to gratefully acknowledge Lamar Hoover for granting me permission to reprint the poem "Momma," which appears on page 109 (from *Momma: a start on all the untold stories*, by Alta. Ojai, California 93024: Times Change Press, P.O. Box 1380, © 1974. Reprinted by permission of the publisher. All rights reserved.). The excerpt from the children's book *A House is a House for Me* that appears on page 97 is also reprinted with the permission of the publisher (From A HOUSE IS A HOUSE FOR ME by Mary Ann Hoberman. Copyright © 1978 by Mary Ann Hoberman. Used by permission of Viking Penguin, a division of Penguin Books USA Inc.).

But, above all, this book belongs to my husband, Rich Goldstein, and to my sons Sam and Noah. Everything I know about love, about intimacy, commitment, and passion, I learned from my life with them.

# Table of Contents

Introduction .......................................................................... 1

Chapter One:    Why Love? ................................................. 7

Chapter Two:    Living Loving Teaching ............................... 37

Chapter Three:  Teacherly Love and Motherly Love ............. 67

Chapter Four:   Mothers and Teachers ................................ 101

Chapter Five:   Collaboration, Relationship, and Love
                in Feminist Research ..................................... 123

Chapter Six:    Issues in Teaching with Love ....................... 149

References ........................................................................... 169

Index .................................................................................. 187

# Introduction

The education of young children is an endeavor dominated by women practitioners. Recent data indicate that 84.9 percent of all elementary school teachers (National Education Association 1993) and 97 percent of all pre-kindergarten teachers are women (National Center for the Early Childhood Workforce 1993). Yet despite this strong association of women educators and young children, there have been few connections made between early childhood education and feminist theory or thinking. Feminist writers on education tend to focus on issues relating to adult learners, while early childhood educators tend to draw on more traditional sources of information, such as developmental psychology and curriculum studies, to inform their practice. Although there are some reasonable explanations for this chasm (see Goldstein 1993; Grumet 1988), it remains puzzling. And it gives rise to an intriguing question: what contribution could feminist thinking make to early childhood educational practices?

There are many answers to this question: feminism has myriad faces, each of which could represent a valuable contribution to the education of young children. This book is just one attempt—my personal attempt—to bring together these two seemingly disparate fields of study, feminist thinking and early childhood education. Its setting is one small place where the two fields meet, a crowded, sunny classroom in a Northern California suburb, in which two teachers, Martha George[1] and myself, set about trying to create and to live a feminism-inspired early childhood education.

The starting point for this feminist vision of early childhood education is feminist moral theory and the ethic of care. The ethic of care's emphasis on "care, concern, and connection" (Martin 1990, 24) is closely aligned with the fundamental values of early childhood education. But in many ways it seems to fall short: the

---

[1]I have used pseudonyms to protect the privacy of the teachers, administrators, children, and parents mentioned in this study.

term "ethic of care" feels academic-sounding, dry, and impersonal, somehow lacking the passion and the commitment that characterize the experience of teaching young children; it is a buzzword lifted from a scholar's phrasebook; it does not belong to the mothertongue, the language of schools, children, and teachers. Given my desire to explore feminist theory in a classroom filled with children, I needed to translate this lofty term into a phrase more accessible, more vital, better suited to classroom life. I needed something warm, moist, human. I needed a word that kids could understand. I needed a notion that would draw on feminist thinking and yet still embody the essence of early childhood education. So I opted to use the word "love." Love was the right word, I thought. It seemed to say it all. It is a term that is both useful and powerful, one that is commonly used by teachers but unexplored by academics and scholars. I knew that love might take me into uncharted territory but, inspired by the feminist spirit of honesty, I felt unafraid.

In order to explore the contributions made by love to the teaching of young children, I entered into a collaborative research and teaching relationship with Martha George, a primary grade teacher whose teaching practices exemplify what I have come to call teaching with love. During a three-month period, I was a daily participant in the life of Martha's kindergarten-first-second grade classroom. I was an observer, then a participant, and finally a full-fledged teaching partner, observing and reflecting upon the role of love in Martha's teaching and in my own. I also examined the impact of our love-based philosophies of education on our team-teaching experience. Given the feminist genealogy of this study, it was important to us to develop a research methodology that would embody feminist perspectives and values. We attempted to engage lovingly in our research endeavors, just as we engage lovingly in our work with children. In feminist scholarship, as in high quality early childhood education, consistency and principles matter.

Of course, it must be noted that both "feminism" and "early childhood education" are somewhat slippery terms that tend to be used in many different contexts with many different meanings. Although I hope to make connections between early childhood education and feminism, I realize that not all early childhood educators are women, nor are they all feminists. I do not intend to create rigid categories or to exclude any interested early childhood practitioners. In fact, it is difficult and problematic to use the word feminism at all—as if it were a monolithic entity rather than a blanket term that encompasses many different and equally valid feminisms. Thus it is necessary to make clear what I mean by the term feminism, as well as by the term early childhood education, and to say a few words about how they will be used in this book.

First, both terms have their generic definitions. Feminism, it would be generally agreed, is a social movement that intends to call attention to the oppression of women and, ultimately, to put an end to it (Narayan 1989; Mies 1991; Farganis 1989; and many others). The field of early childhood education, according to The National Association for the Education of Young Children (Bredekamp 1987), encompasses both the custodial care and the education of children from birth through age eight. These generic definitions will be used throughout this book whenever I am speaking generally on these two topics.

At other times, however, these terms will have more specific—and more personal—meanings. I acknowledge the validity of the generic definition of feminism. However, in my view, not all work that deals with women's inequality in society is feminist, and not all feminist work deals directly with women and oppression. My personal definition of feminism, the one that colors this work and informs my thinking, dives deeply into feminist moral theory, and is rooted in my own experience as a mother, a woman, a scholar, and a teacher of young children. I define feminism as a critical perspective that values ideas, positions, and ways of knowing and thinking that have traditionally been considered female: caring, emotion, intuition, connection, and interdependence, for example. This working definition of feminism is decidedly and deliberately transformative, but is not hostile or exclusionary. In reference to the works of authors who identify themselves as feminists, the more generic definition of feminism may be in order: it is certainly broader and more general. When I speak of my own feminism, however, this is the definition to which I refer.

In many ways, educating is an act of caregiving, regardless of the age of the students. In the field of early childhood education, in particular, it is impossible to tease apart the twin strands of education and care; this is especially true with the youngest children. The staff at my son Sam's infant-toddler day care center referred to themselves both as teachers and as caregivers with little distinction: the field has even coined the neologism "educarers" (Gerber 1979) to represent the interwoven nature of these responsibilities. Nevertheless, in the context of this book I have focused primarily on the role of love in the educational practices of early childhood education—pedagogy, curriculum, classroom organization and management, assessment, and so on.

What is the purpose of bringing the fields of feminism and early childhood education together? Simply put, this symbiotic partnership makes good sense for both fields. Contemporary feminism, rooted in the consciousness-raising tradition of the 1970s, has always had a strong focus on adult experience. This would not be a problem were it not for feminism's transformative vision. Feminists (if it is possible to generalize about such a diverse group) aspire to improve the world—to make it a fairer, kinder, and more humane place for all people. Education, particularly the education of young people, would play a crucial role in such social change. Feminist education cannot afford to ignore children any longer.

And early childhood education cannot afford to ignore feminism. It is easy to forget that for centuries of human existence, early childhood education was a woman-centered act, a mother's work, done in the home with a curriculum of love and care. The twentieth-century emphasis on science as a source of theoretical authority has obscured early childhood education's feminist roots. Reuniting early childhood education with a loving feminist perspective would serve to reverse the scientifically oriented, developmental psychology–driven paradigm that has dominated the profession since the Progressive Era (Bloch 1987) and which has recently come under sharp critique (see Kessler and Swadener 1992). Looking to feminist scholarship as a source of theoretical authority would give women a voice in a field they have dominated in silence. My hope is that this book will provide insight into one of the many possible feminist contributions to early childhood education, and will provide inspiration for all of us who consider ourselves both feminists and teachers of young children.

Chapter One serves as an introduction to the idea of teaching with love. The feminist roots of loving teaching are made clear in a detailed discussion of the ethic of care as well as of other feminist visions of education that have been developed in its wake. In this chapter I define love for the purposes of this study, elaborate on some of the critical issues raised by the notion of teaching with love, and describe the ways Martha and I designed our study to reflect our commitment to love in teaching and learning.

A narrative portrait of teaching with love, Chapter Two is a case study of Martha George's teaching in her K-1-2 classroom, and provides specific details about the ways in which love can contribute both to the educational experiences of children and to the professional experiences of early childhood educators.

Chapter Three focuses on my own experiences as a loving teacher. Drawing on feminist traditions of autobiography as well as on recent developments in teacher research, this case study depicts the challenges of being simultaneously a mother and a teacher of young children, explores the tensions inherent in pursuing collaborative research in another woman's classroom, and lays bare the deeply emotional nature of teaching young children with love.

In Chapter Four an essential theme that has already emerged clearly in Chapters Two and Three—the complicated, charged relationships between mothers and teachers—receives the close analysis it requires, since it would be short-sighted indeed to talk about the nature and character of loving teaching relationships with children without examining the child's first loving teaching relationship: with his/her mother. This chapter explores the literature on motherhood and mothering and on the gendered nature of relationships between mothers and teachers, and relates it to vignettes from life in Martha George's classroom. The chapter concludes with a description and discussion of motherly love and teacherly love.

Adopting a feminist perspective on early childhood teaching suggests that we might also want to consider bringing other aspects of feminist scholarship into the realm of early childhood educational research. Chapter Five takes a thorough look at feminist research methodologies, examining both their pleasures and their pitfalls as revealed within the context of this study. This chapter explores relational issues in Martha's and my collaborative research relationship, and offers methodological insights of potential value not only for feminist researchers but for all scholars interested in collaborative research.

The final chapter explores the main themes of teaching with love that emerged across the three case studies. Issues relating to the dark side of love in classroom settings—ambivalence, dangers, and complications—are raised and discussed. The chapter concludes with a return to the ethic of care and an analysis of the value and utility of teaching with love for feminists, for early childhood educators, and for those who proudly consider themselves to be both.

# 1
# Why Love?

Teachers often speak about loving their students. "The little girl...
was colorless and I didn't have very much feeling for her for a long
time," one teacher reports. "Then all of a sudden when she began
to make discoveries, her personality popped out and I loved her"
(anonymous teacher cited in Jackson 1968/1990, 139). Anna
Tiant, a teacher in an infant-toddler day care center, states
plainly: "What's important to very young kids is to be loved, to
be safe, to be cared for, and that's what I do. The toddler
curriculum is a curriculum of love" (Tiant, cited in Ayers 1989,
24). My conversations with teachers in classrooms, staff rooms,
faculty lounges, play yards, rest rooms, and parking lots at day
care centers, preschools, and elementary schools around the
country suggest that love for students is an underlying assumption
of the practices of many, many early childhood teachers.

Teachers of older students also experience these loving
feelings. Jaime Escalante, the well-known mathematics teacher
depicted in the film *Stand and Deliver*, asserts: "I exhibit deep
love and caring for my students. I have no exclusive claim to these
attributes; they are as natural as breathing to most teachers"
(1990, 9).

Academics, too, take teacherly love for students to be a
commonplace of education. Bill Ayers (1989), for example,
asserts that loving children is an essential qualification for
preschool teachers, and that each young child has a right to be
loved and understood in his or her school setting. Philip Jackson
(1968/1990, 29) writes that "we know that a child's relationship
with his teacher can at times rival in intensity the union between
him and his mother and father," and notes that many of the
teachers he spoke with while researching his landmark book *Life in
Classrooms* revealed their deep affection for and emotional
attachment to their students. In a recent address to the
Association for Supervision and Curriculum Development, Cornel

West described teachers as people who "care so deeply and love so much" (West 1996).

Despite all this acknowledgment, there has been no research undertaken on exactly how love operates in the classroom lives of teachers and children. Teacherly love is present, as the quotes I have cited indicate, but it is somehow invisible, transparent, something that has been taken for granted and deemed unworthy of scholarly attention. Everyone seems to know that teachers love their students—it is a given, as fundamental a part of elementary classroom life as the feel of perpetually dull pencils textured by anonymous toothmarks and the ghoulish light emanating from the ever-buzzing fluorescent lights overhead. Teacherly love is obvious. Why investigate the obvious?

Another reason for the lack of systematic inquiry into this topic is that teacherly love is problematic from a research standpoint. It is mushy, fuzzy, subjective, personal, loaded. In a word, unresearchable. No one has turned the lens of scholarly inquiry to focus on the dimensions and nature of teacherly love because wise scholars tend to shy away from unresearchable research topics. Love is difficult to define, impossible to measure, and outside the boundaries of generalizability, reliability, and validity. Why bother?

Teacherly love has the distinction of being both too obvious to study and too difficult to study. But it is too important to ignore.

My own interest in love in education is rooted in my lived experience as a primary grade teacher. As Chapter Three will illustrate, loving my young students was a basic component of my teaching practices. When I left classroom teaching to pursue a scholarly career, I learned that I was not alone in my deep commitment to the primacy of caring relationships: a raft of scholars before me had already begun to articulate what I had felt all along. Feminist psychologists and philosophers were busy carving out a place for caring, connection, and emotion in scholarly life.

Eager to find out more about feminist perspectives as they related to the education of young children, I headed off to the library. I found a fair number of books about feminist pedagogy and feminist educational theory. But none of them took into consideration the concerns, issues, and challenges of early childhood education. This seemed odd: early childhood education is a field dominated by women teachers, and caring relationships are a hallmark of life in classrooms with young children. Feminism and early childhood education seemed like natural partners.

I complained and fretted about the disconnection between these two disciplines. The university librarians heard about it, my colleagues heard about it, my students heard about it, my friends heard about it. I worried about how I would ever be able to do research on this topic if there were no books available on the subject. This went on for several days, until I recalled a passage written by Alice Walker in which she describes one facet of her motivation to write: "In my own work I write not only what I want to read—understanding fully and indelibly that if I don't do it no one else is so vitally interested, or capable of doing it to my satisfaction—I write all the things *I should have been able to read*" (Walker 1983, 13). Walker helped me to realize that I would have to be the one to write a book on the intersections of feminism and early childhood education. What you are about to read is that book. Using the feminist ethic of care as a starting point, I explore some of the possibilities and some of the variety that characterize the love that some/many/most/all early childhood teachers feel for the students in their care.

### Feminist theory, the ethic of care, and love

There are multiple feminist perspectives, and many ways to be a feminist. However, there are several essential elements at the core of feminist thinking. Feminist theory is based on the observation that women have been oppressed and devalued by the patriarchal bias of our society (Narayan 1989; Mies 1991; Farganis 1989). Feminists believe that women must be empowered, and advocate the acknowledgment, affirmation, and celebration of women, women's experiences, and women's perspectives. Women have traditionally been marginalized in our culture, but feminists place women and women's ways of knowing (Belenky, Clinchy, Goldgerber, and Tarule 1986) at the center of their world view. Finally, feminist theory is transformative: it "provides groundwork for our collective effort to recast and remake the world" (Fisher 1987, 23). Feminists envision a future in which women's voices, and all marginalized voices, will be respected and heard.

Feminists assert that the "information" and "facts" that form the foundation of Western knowledge are not objective truths. That information was recorded by men, reflected the perspective of men, and focused mainly on the experiences of men (Maher 1983). This has given men exclusive power and ownership over certain types of high-prestige knowledge. Feminist scholars (and others including postpositivist philosophers and postmodernists) have pointed out that what has generally been labelled "the truth" actually represents only a fraction of the reality of any given historical moment. The world view commonly presented as universal can no longer be considered universal. As an antidote to the traditional androcentric views of the world espoused by generations of male scholars (and female scholars working in male-dominated fields of inquiry), feminist scholars have offered dramatic reinterpretations of history presented from the perspective of women.[2] By attending to the experiences of women, feminists have encouraged all scholars to recognize that both male and female experiences are varied and specific, thus challenging the notion of universality (Maher 1985). Further, in exposing the flaws of our commonly held assumptions, feminism calls for a critical examination and reevaluation of all our paradigms.

By questioning the existence of objective knowledge, feminism directs its scholarly energies into the realm of the subjective. Feminist scholarship provides evidence that different people, because of the specifics of their life situations and experiences, have different understandings of "reality" (Fisher 1987). Further, feminism actively values the knowledge embodied in personal experience. Feminist scholarship is characterized by an emphasis on personal experience and personal perspectives, a reflection of the familiar feminist slogan that "the personal is political." As an alternative to the notion of objective truth, feminist philosophers have called for intersubjectivity, the creation of an aggregate of subjectivities. By taking into account as many different

---

[2]For an example of this type of research, see Joan Kelly's "Did Women Have a Renaissance?" in Bridenthal and Koonz, eds. *Becoming Visible: Women in European History* (Boston: Houghton Mifflin, 1977).

perspectives and experiences as are relevant, feminists aim to construct a picture of the world that is as full and rich as possible.

Feminist scholarship requires more than a simple shifting of subject matter, analyzing women instead of men. It involves adopting a specific critical stance, developing a different understanding of knowledge, and engaging in a process intended to critique and transform academic disciplines and, ultimately, society. One discipline that has been the object of sustained feminist scrutiny is moral theory. Scholarship in the field now known as feminist ethics began with a simple shifting of focus, looking away from men to attend to the perspectives and experiences of women. From that starting point, transformative notions emerged.

The traditional vein of moral theory, rooted in the works of Kant and Locke (Kittay and Meyers 1987), presumes a commitment to personal liberty and individual autonomy. Reason leads to universal codes for behavior. Moral decisions are made according to rigid and unbending principles. This perspective is clearly visible in the work of Lawrence Kohlberg (1981). He suggests that moral development proceeds in a series of clearly articulated stages. People begin by simply deferring to authority (stage 1), then learn to make decisions that will satisfy their own needs (stage 2). Next, they act out of a desire to please others (stage 3), augmented by a commitment to maintain the social order (stage 4). As they mature, people learn to associate morality with the accepted values of their society (stage 5). Ultimately, when people reach the most sophisticated level of moral reasoning (stage 6), they make decisions based on universal principles of justice. These stages of development are hierarchical: moral maturity is attained at stage 6, and all of the preceding levels are less complete. Not all adults attain stage 6, though all should aspire to. Kohlberg, steeped in the philosophical traditions of moral theory, posited that the most sophisticated manner of making moral decisions is by calling upon universal principles, invoking the language of rights and justice.

In a landmark feminist work, *In a Different Voice* (1982), Carol Gilligan addressed Kohlberg's stages head-on. Gilligan noted that men and women seemed to have different scoring patterns in terms of placement in Kohlberg's stages. Women, even well-educated and intelligent women, seemed to get stuck at stage 3, where morality is associated with doing what seems "right" in the eyes of others; men tended to move to Stage 4 or even beyond. As a result, Kohlberg's work intimated that women were not as moral as men, or, at best, simply not as well developed. In keeping with feminist scholarship's commitment to transformation, Gilligan transformed the argument. She asserted that Kohlberg's scale was developed by examining the experiences and decision making of men. As a result, Kohlberg's work was not truly a theory of moral development, but simply a theory of male moral development. Women received "low" scores on Kohlberg's scale because the scale was inappropriate for measuring the moral lives of women. Gilligan maintained that women's moral stature was not inferior to men's; it was qualitatively different from men's.

Gilligan did not take issue with Kohlberg's placement of women at stage 3, making moral decisions in ways that would enable them to please others. Her point was that this is not a problem, a sign of immaturity, or a failure to develop. She had found in her research that women make decisions in ways that enable them to maintain relationships, and to sustain connection, using a type of reasoning distinctly different from that implied by traditional moral theory, in which good decisions are made in accordance with universal principles. Gilligan found that abstract principles were fairly irrelevant: the women she studied tended to take contextual factors into account, and were neither able nor willing to reduce complex situations to simple black and white. She asserted that Kohlberg's stages simply fail to capture women's concerns and strategies.

Gilligan does not denounce the utility of hierarchical scales of moral development, but seeks to complement Kohlberg's stages with a parallel developmental scale that better represents women's experiences. Women's moral reasoning, Gilligan suggests, develops along a distinct and different path. Beginning at or around Kohlberg's stage 3, women move from an orientation that focuses simply on serving others toward a greater emphasis on self-actualization. At all points on this path, however, the commitment to sustaining relationships remains strong and central.

In proposing an alternative model of moral development—an ethic of responsibility in contrast to a morality of rights (Gilligan 1982, 164)—Gilligan gave women permission to let their hearts play an active role in their thinking. Women no longer had faulty moral reasoning, or minds fettered by pesky emotions. Instead, women's reasoning seemed both careful and care-full, deliberately valuing human interaction and experience. Many women (myself very much included) cheered, wept, and sighed with relief as we read *In a Different Voice*. Gilligan held up a mirror, allowing us see ourselves at last.

Scholars, even feminist scholars, have since poked holes in Gilligan's work. A 1986 forum in the academic journal *Signs* raised a great many concerns. Gilligan's research was characterized by dangerous oversimplification (Kerber 1986), and was not rigorous enough to be convincing (Greeno and Maccoby 1986). There were serious methodological issues: the sample size was too small, there was inconsistent coding of interview responses, the overall approach was too impressionistic (Luria 1986). And the work was deeply flawed by its cultural myopia, paying no attention at all to issues of race and class in moral reasoning (Stack 1986). Other critics were concerned with Gilligan's willingness to leave out the historical context in which discussions of men's and women's differences must be embedded (Nicholson 1983), and with her misinterpretation of Kohlberg's data: Walker (1984) examined 61 studies done with Kohlberg's methods and found no significant scoring difference linked to gender.[3]

However, despite all of these valid criticisms, it would be a mistake to underestimate the powerful impact of *In a Different Voice*. By calling into question the universality of moral principles and giving primacy to connection and concern, Gilligan opened the door to further inquiry into the nature of women's ways of thinking about the world and their experiences in it. Her work was followed by a powerful flow of feminist writing on issues in ethics. The authors of these works on what is now known as the ethic of care intended to "develop a feminist moral theory to deal with the regions of experience that have been central to women's experience and neglected by traditional moral theory" (Held 1987, 114).

The most profoundly influential proponent of the ethic of care is Nel Noddings, author of the germinal work *Caring* (1984). When Noddings uses the term caring, she is describing not an

---

[3]Diana Baumrind (1986) asserts that Walker's examination of Kohlberg's data is seriously flawed: her reexamination of the same data suggest that in fact there are sex-linked differences in scoring patterns.

attribute or personality trait, but a relation. Caring is not something you are, but rather something you engage in, something you do. Every interaction provides one with an opportunity to enter into a caring relation, although, certainly, individuals always retain the option of interacting in either a caring or an uncaring way. Noddings asserts the deep moral dimension of her own personal relationship to the ethic of care: "My first and unending obligation is to meet the other as one-caring" (1984, 17).

As Noddings describes it, each caring encounter is an interaction between a person giving care and a person receiving that care: a one-caring and a cared-for. (For the sake of clarity I will refer to the one-caring with the pronoun "she" and the cared-for with the pronoun "he." Of course, individuals of either sex can fill either role in the caring relation.) In a caring encounter, the one-caring meets the cared-for with engrossment. The one-caring opens herself to the cared-for with full attention, and with receptivity to his perspective and situation. The one-caring's stance is further characterized by her motivational displacement, defined by Noddings as the willingness to give primacy, even if momentarily, to the goals and needs of the cared-for. This combination of engrossment and motivational displacement can happen on many different levels, from the intense—a mother caring for an infant—to the fleeting—a stranger on campus stopping a busy professor to ask for directions. Though it is easy to envision the mother-infant relation as caring, the second scenario is equally well explained as a caring encounter using Noddings's definitions and terminology. The busy professor pauses, listening carefully to the request of the stranger (Noddings's engrossment). She has temporarily ceased her own musings and given primacy to the pressing needs of the stranger (Noddings's motivational displacement). Noddings puts it simply: "Caring involves stepping out of one's own personal frame of reference and into the other's" (1984, 24). It is the engrossment and motivational displacement that are the hallmarks of caring, not the depth of feeling.

After the one-caring and the cared-for interact, the caring encounter is completed once the cared-for has acknowledged the care he has received. This reciprocity is the sole role of the cared-for in a caring relation. Reciprocity can take different forms—a smile from a baby, a thank you from the lost stranger—but it must occur in every caring encounter.

In mature healthy relationships, all involved parties get the opportunity to be both the one-caring and the cared-for. The mother-infant relationship, however, is an exception. It is bound to be very one-sided: the mother is always the one-caring and the infant always the cared-for. Yet their caring encounters are mutually satisfying. Noddings writes: "In every caring encounter the mother is necessarily carer and the infant cared-for. But the infant responds—he or she coos, wriggles, stares attentively, smiles, reaches out, and cuddles. These responses are heartwarming; they make caregiving a rewarding experience" (1992, 17). These caring encounters are also learning experiences for the infant. It is by being the cared-for that he or she will learn how to be one-caring.

This perspective has significant implications for schooling. Teachers who meet their students as ones-caring, and who look upon the act of teaching as an opportunity to participate in caring encounters, will be teaching their students more than academic knowledge. These children will have the opportunity to learn how to care. This is more than the mere modelling of desired behaviors. It is a moral stance that has the potential to transform education.

Feminist ethicists, philosophers, and psychologists link this ethic of care with women, women's ways of knowing, and women's experiences. Doing so raises the specter of essentialism. Are all women caring? Must women be caring? Can men be caring? Further, some feminists denounce the ethic of care (Card 1990; Hoagland 1990; Houston 1990; Tronto 1989, among others). Portraying women as carers traps women in an oppressive, stereotyped, and tradition-bound set of roles and behaviors. Caring perpetuates inequality and subjugation.

However, I believe that rooting this perspective squarely in experience, as Noddings has done, allows women to own caring in a way that makes it a strength rather than a weakness. It is the experience of giving and receiving care that leads to a caring perspective on moral decision making. Were more men involved in the giving and receiving of care as an ongoing, central, and valued part of their lives, they would be as likely to espouse this viewpoint as women are. Giving up the ethic of care, allowing patriarchal power to take caring from us, would itself be a form of oppression.

Though Nel Noddings's caring is its most well-known face, the ethic of care has been articulated and elaborated upon by many different scholars, and is known by many names. Each scholar has drawn on evidence from a variety of perspectives and fields of inquiry and made her case thoughtfully and thoroughly, choosing her terminology with deliberate care. And while there are definite differences among these iterations, explorations, and explications of the ethic of care, they are deeply similar in significant ways. To summarize this feminist position, Jane Roland Martin has coined the catchy phrase "the 3 Cs"—care, concern, and connection (1990, 24).

The 3 Cs are the intellectual foundation upon which my vision of loving teaching is built. However, one essential element needs to be added to them in order to bring them to life for the field of early childhood education: passion. The ethic of care is a highly complex and subtle web of words and emotions, but it lacks the fire, the spark, the ebullient energy that is required to teach young children with love. Mem Fox, the well-known Australian children's author and literacy expert, describes an experience in which passion proved to be the key element in teaching a three-year-old boy to read. The important question, she asserts, is not about the text or the method:

> The important question, I believe, is: what happened between me and the child?
> What happened was a frenzy of silliness and excited game playing, with me shouting and laughing and saying: "Yes! Yes! Yes!" in higher and higher tones, and hugging Ben who was laughing and grinning as if this *reading* thing were just about the best fun he'd ever had. We were rolling around the floor literally, and banging the book with our hands at each new revelation of "It's time for bed," shrieking in triumph as the words were revealed on each page.
> We were never tense. We were never quiet. Even when we were looking for and finding the same farm animals in each book, we were noisy and wild in our discoveries.
> "There's ANOTHER pig. Oh no! ANOTHER horse! And look, there's a cow in this book, and a cow in this book and another cow in THIS book!!! Can you believe it? Cows, cows, everywhere!"
> Ben's face was alight. I could have eaten him, he was so adorable and so smart; and of course he thought I was pretty special too, every time I lifted him off the floor in a giant hug and said: "Ooooh, you're so CLEVER!" We could have played with books for hours. We didn't want to stop. Good grief! How happy we were. (1995, 5–6)

Of course, we are not all Mem Fox. Her story tells more about who she is as a person and as a teacher than it does about how to teach children to read. But it conveys quite clearly both the type of passion that I feel is missing from the ethic of care and the importance of passion in teaching young children. Maxine Greene (1986, 81), another advocate of passion in teaching, writes: "An emotion, a passion can be a transformation of the world. It can break through the fixities; it can open to the power of possibility."

I define this marriage of passion to care, concern, and connection as "love." However, in many ways, I am hesitant to define love too precisely or too concretely. There is much about love's role in classroom life that I cannot hope to know, since I have only been deeply involved in the life of a small handful of loving classrooms. In this study I looked closely and carefully at the role that love plays in the professional practices of two teachers. My goal was not to prove that love exists in these educational settings: the teachers that I studied, Martha George and myself, have stated outright that love is an important factor in our teaching and in the lives of our classrooms. Instead, this study moves beyond those statements into an exploration of the nature of teaching with love and the various contributions that love can make to the education of young children. In order to do this, it is important to have some sense of what other scholars have found when looking at love.

Love has been described as "an unescapable reality in American thought" (Varenne 1977, 195). Everyone knows what love is, and the "feeling of meaningless repetition and uniformity" (Varenne 1977, 195) that surrounds the word suggests that it is a topic well defined and widely researched. Yet that is not the case. In his book *Americans Together* (1977), sociologist Herve Varenne looks at the role of love in community discourse in America, and describes himself as one of the first to systematically study the concept and role of love in our culture and our cultural structures.

Love has, of course, been well documented and exhaustively explored by psychologists; nevertheless, as virtually all of the scientific research done on love has focused exclusively on heterosexual, adult-adult romantic/erotic love (Sternberg 1988b), there has been little inquiry into the specific nature of the many other loving relationships people encounter in their daily lives. Most notably absent, for the purposes of this study, is research on parent-child love[4]: I suspect that this is the type of love that most closely resembles the relationship between a loving teacher and her students.

The work of psychologist Robert Sternberg (1988a; 1988b) provides a useful model of love, and one that I believe holds great promise for the understanding of love in classrooms: unlike the many models and analyses of love that emphasize attraction and arousal (which I do not review or discuss here, in view of their irrelevance to the task at hand), Sternberg's model can be applied honestly to nonsexual varieties of love. Though clearly not designed for this purpose, Sternberg's model, with only slight modifications, can be applied to the teacherly love I explored and experienced in this study.

Sternberg calls his model "the triangular theory of love" (1988a), and suggests that love be understood in terms of three components—intimacy, commitment, and passion—that form the three sides of a triangle (see Figure 1).

Intimacy, in Sternberg's words, describes "the close, connected, and bonded feelings in loving relationships" (1988a, 120); commitment entails both the decision to love someone and the commitment to maintain that love; and passion is "the drives that lead to romance, physical attraction, sexual consummation and the like" (1988a, 120).

In applying this model to adult-adult loving relationships, Sternberg sees a variety of subsets of love, each involving a different proportion of these three factors. Intimacy alone, for example, leads to liking; intimacy and passion—without commitment——lead to romantic love; intimacy and commitment devoid of passion lead to companionate love; and so on. Sternberg also suggests that satisfying relationships are ones in which the partners' triangles are similarly shaped, balanced (or unbalanced, as the case may be) along similar sides, and in which the levels of intensity (represented by the area of the triangle) are the same for both partners. Finally, he asserts that these triangles change over time; and that the success of relationships depends upon the adaptability of people to these inevitable changes.

---

[4]The bulk of the scientific work done so far on mothers and children has focused on attachment behaviors (Ainsworth 1978; Bowlby 1966; Harlow 1986). Urie Bronfenbrenner (1970; 1979) looks at the importance of loving interactions within the caregiver-child dyad, but does not specifically analyze the nature or dimensions of mother-child love.

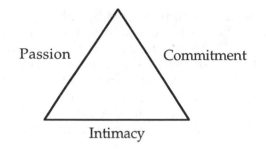

Figure 1

I would suggest that Sternberg's three components of love—intimacy, commitment, and passion—defined in slightly different ways, accurately describe the type of love experienced by teachers who create loving educational environments.  In my version of Sternberg's triangle, intimacy still represents those "close, connected, and bonded feelings" that are found in loving relationships, but the concept must be writ large enough to move from a one-on-one setting to the sort of large-scale intimacy that is impossible anywhere but a classroom.  Intimacy embodies trust, the sharing of meaningful experiences, a degree of mutuality and reciprocity among participants, a commitment to open communication, and a depth of feeling regardless of the number of people participating in the relationship.  Sometimes a teacher experiences this type of intimacy with a single student—at a one-on-one writing conference, for example—but it can also be experienced by a teacher with a whole class, and even by the class as a community, with the teacher as a member of the larger body.  Sternberg's intimacy component also covers some of the same ground as the ethic of care, with its emphasis on caring, concern, and connection.

Commitment is a crucial part of a teacher's professional life: commitment to the students and to the subject matter being taught should be a fundamental part of a teacher's responsibility.  Teachers commit time, effort, and resources to their preparations and their teaching (Hargreaves 1994; Lortie 1975).  Teachers also have to make a commitment to their students.  In her research on primary teachers, Nias (1989, 31) found that "commitment" is the term that teachers themselves use to distinguish "real teachers" from those who do not take the job seriously:  it is a crucial part of a teacher's professional sense of self.

The commitment component of Sternberg's triangular model, which he describes as the decision to love and to maintain that love, seems well suited to teacherly love. In applying this commitment component to the case of loving education, the teacher would move a step beyond the most fundamental professional commitments and enter in addition into a commitment to engage in a loving relationship with all of her students and to attempt to uphold that love, even if it is unrequited.

Passion, Sternberg's final component, is the most dangerous to take at face value: it is too sexually charged to apply directly to discussions of teaching and teacherly love. Under no circumstances is it appropriate for a classroom teacher to be driven toward romance, physical attraction, sexual consummation and the like in her relationships with students, especially in early childhood educational settings. And yet passion, albeit in a different form, plays an important role in excellent teaching—and, by extension, in loving education. It is this component of Sternberg's triangular model that needs to be redefined for use in the description of teacherly love.

The American College Dictionary defines "passion" as any kind of feeling or emotion, when of compelling force. Thinking of passion as a driving force that compels action eliminates the sexual connotations that often surround the word. In the context of teaching with love, passion could be defined as a teacher's compelling desire to teach, to work with children, and to facilitate interactions between children and content.

The idea of passion playing a role in teaching is not new. In his essay "Men Without Chests," C.S. Lewis (1953) explores the role of emotions in education. He roots his thinking in the ancient Greek notion of the chest as the seat of all that is truly human: "It may even be said that it is by this middle element that man is man: for by his intellect he is mere spirit and by his appetite mere animal"(16). He ends by warning against any form of education that creates "men without chests," thus emphasizing the importance of feelings, emotions, and passions in schooling.

Passion has recently returned to the forefront of our discourse about schooling in the work of Robert Fried. An advocate of school reform strategies aimed at inspiring, engaging, and motivating students, Fried points to passionate teachers and passionate teaching as the essential elements in the equation. He writes: "To be a passionate teacher is to be someone in love with a field of knowledge, deeply stirred by issues and ideas that challenge our world, drawn to the dilemmas and potentials of the young people who come into class each day" (Fried 1995, 1). Fried asserts that "it is this quality of caring about ideas and values, this fascination with the potential for growth within people, this depth and fervor about doing things well and striving for excellence" (Fried 1995, 17) that sets the passionate teachers apart from the rest of their profession.

Building on Fried's excellent work, I would add that a passionate teacher is energized by her life with her students, and feels fulfilled by her work with them. A passionate teacher teaches with joy, from her heart. This form of passion is intense but not sexual. It is similar to the passion that artists feel toward their work, or that parents feel toward their children. Mem Fox's story about reading with little Ben offers an excellent example of passionate teaching.

In loving teaching, then, I expect to find all three of these components—intimacy, commitment, and passion—playing out in ways that are specific to the teacher and students and setting being observed. When all three components are present in a relationship, Sternberg calls it "consummate love" (1988a, 122). And while it may be possible to find excellent teachers who do not feel love for their students, I think that if love is to be present in a classroom, it has to be present in this consummate form. Though Sternberg does not state this explicitly, I believe that it is important to note that the whole of consummate love is greater than the simple sum of its three parts: there is something else, something intangible and magical, that results from the balanced interaction of passion, commitment and intimacy. One of the purposes of this study is to examine the nature of this type of consummate love in educational settings.

## Love and the education of young children

Love was the heart of the curriculum of early childhood education for many centuries. Mothers were the sole providers of education to young children, and the home was the primary educational setting. Raising and educating children has traditionally been a responsibility of women, and seen as a fundamental facet of mothering. By extension, the education of young children has also been seen as women's work.

Though the field of early childhood education is dominated by women practitioners, the theoretical authority it has been based on has come not from maternal practices, but from the science of developmental psychology (Goldstein 1993), long the driving force behind research and practice in the field (Walsh 1993; Bloch 1992; Kessler 1991a). Its influence is profound and pervasive. While the alliance between developmental psychology and early childhood education is certainly not monolithic or uniform (Spodek 1989a)—the dominant conceptions in both reflect dramatically different viewpoints—but when educational programs for young children are classified or described, it is generally the theories of mind and learning forming a program that determine where it will be placed.

For example, Kohlberg and Mayer refer to three views of human development that manifest themselves in the field of early childhood education: cultural transmission, romantic, and progressive. The cultural transmission model is as old as the "classical academic tradition of Western education" (1972, 453). It takes as the purpose of education to enable students to acquire the specific skills and knowledge required for success in life in our society. Skills are taught by direct or indirect means in programs espousing this viewpoint, and are often arranged in a careful, hierarchical progression of steps. The work of behaviorists such as Edward L. Thorndike and B.F. Skinner reflect this orientation, as did many of the programmed learning models of the 1960s.

In direct contrast, the romantic model centers on a belief that education and growth must come from within the child. Originating in the work of Jean-Jacques Rousseau, and exemplified by A.S. Neill and Arnold Gesell, this view supports children developing at their own pace, unfolding organically and naturally. Educators in programs reflecting this orientation have no outcomes in mind other than to provide support for the spontaneous growth of their young students.

The progressive model, drawing on the work of Jean Piaget and John Dewey, is based on the notion that children play an active role in creating their own development. Children move through developmental stages as a result of active thinking about meaningful problems and challenges found in the world around them, and their psychological structures are reorganized with each problem solved.

This last model currently wields the strongest influence in the field, and can be summed up with the phrase "developmentally appropriate practice." Developmentally appropriate practice, as described in a widely influential position paper published by the National Association for the Education of Young Children (NAEYC) (Bredekamp 1987), aims to take into account a child's developmental readiness for any particular task or activity. Teachers engaged in developmentally appropriate practice are sensitive to the particular needs of each child and attempt to create a meaningful, challenging, responsive, and stimulating educational environment for all students, regardless of their location on developmental continua. Children are given opportunities to learn through direct experience and hands-on exploration, and to engage in the kinds of problem-finding and problem-solving that lead to growth and development.

The NAEYC standards for developmentally appropriate practice arose in response to the trend toward pushing the skills-driven academic curriculum of the elementary school down into the classrooms of the very young. This trend has its roots in the the academic achievement frenzy that followed the launch of Sputnik in 1957, and in the compensatory education programs such as Project Head Start launched as part of President Lyndon Johnson's War on Poverty in the mid 1960s. During that period, expanding knowledge of child development, exemplified by Benjamin Bloom's assertion that half of an individual's intelligence can be accounted for in the first four years of life (1964), added fuel to the fire of direct instruction for young children. The educational experiences that resulted from these influences, however, tended to have a profoundly "psychometric" (Elkind 1989) flavor, and generally reflected a behavioristic or cultural transmission philosophy. Developmentally appropriate practice stands as a humane and sensitive alternative to "hurrying" children, i.e., forcing academic activities, like worksheets, phonics drills and flash cards, on children too young to benefit from them (Elkind 1981).

Though it sounds benign, developmentally appropriate practice has recently come under critical scrutiny. Criticisms have taken different forms, ranging from practical applications of educational philosophy (Spodek 1989b; Kessler 1991a) to concern over the artificial separation of cognition and affect (Jipson 1991); from more general critiques of the utility of the notion of broad and universal developmental stages (Walsh 1991) to specific concerns about developmentally appropriate practice's impact on teachers of young children (Jipson 1991); from concerns about issues of equity, fairness, and diversity in the early childhood classroom (Sapon-Shevin 1993; Jipson 1991) to developmentally appropriate practice's focus on children's present state as children rather than on their potential for the future (Kessler 1991b). Many of the critics of developmentally appropriate practice have taken extremely strong stands, dramatically casting new light on practices that most early childhood educators hold as an ideal, or as a standard. Their critiques are intriguing not only because of their content, but because they remind us of the critical importance of constantly rethinking and reevaluating our educational enterprises to improve what we offer our children. The work of these critics has inspired me to think carefully about ways in which early childhood education can be enhanced and improved.

Recent scholarly work in the field of feminist ethics also has direct relevance to the rethinking of early childhood education; these writings characterize women's ways of knowing in terms of relation, interdependence, and caring—the ethic of care—and blend perfectly with the reality of working with young children by building on and further developing the early childhood educator's responsibility to care for young children. Developing this way of thinking into a perspective on educational and curricular decision making would be a significant enhancement of what current practices provide our children and their teachers. In this study I shall explore and develop one possible application of a feminist curriculum theory for early childhood education: teaching with love.

Placing love at the center of an educational enterprise has significant implications. Each educational decision, from placement of the desks to selection of academic content, is made with love for children as the guiding principle. A love-based early childhood curriculum gives a new twist to the teacher's responsibility to act *in loco parentis*. Teachers are no longer being asked simply to act as parents: now they will be expected to enter the feeling and thinking realms of parenthood as well. For example, Mem Fox (1995, 15) issues this request: "I am asking teachers to be as human as parents. Parents . . . are such naturally good teachers that we need to copy what they do and how they behave. We need to emulate the affectionate attitudes and relationships of happy families."

But how do parents think and feel? How do they make their decisions? In her book *Maternal Thinking,*[5] Sara Ruddick (1989) characterizes the three fundaments of parental thought: to preserve the lives of children, to foster their growth, and to shape them according to some ideal of acceptability. Preserving life and fostering growth are already a standard part of most early childhood educational programs: the NAEYC position statement asserts that "a high quality early childhood program provides a safe and nurturing environment that promotes the physical, social, emotional, and cognitive development of young children" (Bredekamp 1987, 1).

But fostering growth makes little sense without a vision of where children should be headed. The NAEYC standards do not address this crucial point. Educational philosophers do: Sara Ruddick writes at length about the challenges inherent in "training a child to be the kind of person whom others accept and whom the mothers themselves can actively appreciate"(1989, 104). John Dewey described the important role of continuity in education: for growth to occur it must build on previous experiences and create conditions that lead to further growth and development (1938). And more recently Nel Noddings addressed the issue head on: "The primary aim of every teacher must be to promote the growth of students as competent, caring, loving, and lovable people"(1992, 154).

Parents and teachers, then, have similar responsibilities, although suggesting that early childhood teachers should think in ways that parents think does not mean that early childhood educators must be parents in order to fully understand their role. Nor do they cease thinking like professionals in the field or return to the old-fashioned maternal model (Bereiter and Engelmann 1966) of teaching young children. While there is a fair amount of overlap between teaching and mothering—Madeleine Grumet has

---

[5]Ruddick employs her own idiosyncratic definition of a mother: "a person who takes on responsibility for children's lives and for whom providing child care is a significant part of her or his working life" (1989, 40). Maternal thinking, then, can be engaged in by men and women alike.

suggested that teaching is "a profession that claimed the colors of motherhood" (1988, 56)—the differences are significant.

Lilian Katz (1981) articulated seven dimensions regarding which mothering and teaching part company: scope of functions, intensity of affect, spontaneity, scope of responsibility, partiality, attachment, and rationality. The scope of a mother's functions is diffuse and limitless. She is never off-duty, and must be concerned at all times about all aspects of her child's life. The purview of teachers, on the other hand, is smaller and more tightly focused. A mother and her child are emotionally invested in one another in a way that leads to a high level of interpersonal intensity. As children struggle toward individuation, mothers and children have inevitable conflicts that teachers and children can avoid.

Katz asserts that mothers are free to be spontaneous, but that teachers must have explicit intentions and careful plans and rationales behind their decisions and actions. Further, a mother is responsible for only one family. Teachers, typically responsible for the children of upwards of thirty families, must deal with a daunting range of cultural differences, expectations, and family values. Katz suggests that teachers should be impartial, in contrast to the partiality of mothers. Her definition of impartiality, that "whatever skills, knowledge, insights, techniques, etc. the teacher has at his or her disposal [are] made equally available to every child *as needed*" (Katz 1981, 18), sounds almost like a recommendation that teachers act as if they were partial to every child. Since it requires teachers to be sensitive to each student's particular needs, impartiality can be subsumed into her "scope of responsibility" dimension.

I find Katz's final dimensions, rationality and attachment, less useful. She suggests that mothers need to be "crazy about their child" (19), while teachers need to employ careful and logical reasoning. This distinction paints a fairly unattractive and unappealing picture of ditsy mothers and mechanistic teachers, and plays upon sexist stereotypes. Further, it reflects a patriarchal assumption that there are two clear-cut categories—rationality and irrationality—and that one is better than the other. On attachment, the final dimension, Katz maintains that mothers and children are engaged in relations of "reciprocal caring," while teachers must maintain "detached concern" (Katz 1981, 15). With this I disagree most heartily. Teachers should avoid being emotionally drained in meeting the needs of the children they teach, but becoming involved in a mutually caring relationship with students is one of the perks of teaching young children. Children and their teachers benefit from such relationships.

Of course, there must be certain boundaries between teaching and mothering.[6] Teachers are certainly not meant to be mother substitutes (Freud 1952), and should avoid becoming involved in rivalries with the mothers of their students. This is damaging to the students and also prevents teachers from carrying out the parent education component of their responsibilities (Bredekamp 1987). Teaching and mothering, just like nursing and mothering, are distinct and separate caring roles that can and should coexist in the lives of young children.

In advocating centering our educational efforts around love and care, I am aware that many early childhood settings are presently not lacking in care. Giving care is a basic, essential part of early childhood education, of the early childhood educator's mandate. But this emotional, interpersonal kernel, which resides at the heart of early childhood education, has never been given any educational authority. Love for children is considered a desirable personality trait for the teachers of the young (Katz 1971), but not a philosophical position, or a basis for educational decision making, which has traditionally drawn upon developmental psychology. Loving early childhood education environments, in direct contrast, would close the gap between what teachers do with children and how they feel about children. They take the love that already exists in many early childhood classrooms and place it on an equal footing with more traditional and official sources of knowledge.

One reason, I suspect, that love for young children has been given little credence as a legitimate scholarly perspective stems from the history of the field of early childhood education. Early in the twentieth century teachers of young children were eager to appear professional, to be deemed experts (Bloch 1987). Caring and love were very nice, but they were not as impressive as scientific knowledge. (In fact, this very criticism has been lobbed at feminist scholars who focus on the subjective, the interpersonal, the experiential rather than the "objective facts" that constitute

---

[6]The boundaries between teaching and mothering, and between teachers and mothers, will be discussed more fully in Chapter Four.

"real" science.)  But caring and love are not nonintellectual acts
(Jaggar 1989).  As Eisner (1982, 20) points out, cognition and
affect cannot be separated:

> This case cannot be made because the hard and fast distinction between
> what is cognitive and what is affective is itself faulty.  In the first place
> there can be no affective activity without cognition.  If to cognize is to
> know, then to have a feeling and not to know it is not to have it.  At the
> very least, in order to have a feeling one must be able to distinguish
> between one state of being and another.  The making of this distinction is
> a product of thinking, a product that itself represents a state of knowing.

Or, in the words of Sara Freedman (1990, 245), "effective
caregiving cannot be divorced from thought, nor productive
thought from caregiving."  Love for children is both an emotional
and an intellectual act, and as such forms a firm foundation on
which to base an early childhood curriculum.

Several feminist scholars have developed models of what
could be called loving education.  Jane Roland Martin (1992)
describes a "schoolhome," an institution that both educates and
gives care to children.  She advocates the notion of "a school as a
moral equivalent of home" (1992, 27), suggesting that this type of
education is becoming increasingly important as the real lives of
American students move further and further from the traditional
nuclear family.  In Martin's schoolhome, children are taught and
nurtured at the same time, making connections with each other,
with academic content, and with the community at large.

Martin begins with a simple rereading of Maria Montessori's
works.  Montessori's phrase "Casa dei Bambini" has generally
been translated in the United States as "The Children's House,"
but Martin asserts that the proper translation should be "The
Children's Home."  This simple semantic shift makes a world of
difference.  Martin goes back and rereads Montessori's writings
and those of "the many pilgrims who travelled to Italy to see
Montessori's schools for themselves" (1992, 10) and finds
evidence that her reading is accurate.  Montessori designed her
schools to function like homes, realizing that for her pupils, some
of Rome's poorest children, school was the most stable and
consistent force in their lives.

For many children today school must play the same role.
Parents are absent, divorced, addicted, or just busy working to try
to make ends meet, and the children's houses are empty, lit only

by the flickering light of the television. And so Martin suggests that many of the traditional responsibilities of the family—support, socialization, moral education, community—have become crucial parts of a child's formal education. When the family does not provide these aspects of education, no one provides them—and the children suffer. The mission of Martin's schoolhome is to pick up the slack, venturing boldly into what was formerly considered the domestic sphere, and radically reshaping education.

The analogous relationship of teaching and parenting discussed earlier forms the foundation for Nel Noddings's vision of feminist education. In *The Challenge to Care in Schools*, Noddings asks the question, "Can we make caring the center of our educational efforts?" (1992, 14), and suggests drawing on a quote from John Dewey: "What the best and wisest parent wants for his own child, that must the community want for all of its children. Any other ideal for our schools is narrow and unlovely; acted upon, it destroys our democracy" (1902/1990, 7). An image emerges of our students as a large heterogeneous family for whom we are responsible; an image which should then be used as a template for making educational decisions.

Noddings further suggests that the standard curriculum of secondary schooling be abandoned and replaced by "domains or centers of caring" (1992, 47). Academic subjects would no longer be segregated into disciplines and taught in isolation. Instead they would be put to use in concert, and taught to children as needed to enable them to solve relevant and interesting educative problems. In Noddings's vision of schooling, children will learn about caring for the self, for others (both in their inner circle and for strangers and distant others), for animals, plants and the earth, for the human-made world and for the world of ideas. She writes: "There clearly are connections that can be made here to the subjects we call history, geography, literature, and science, but I would like those subjects to contribute to centers of care, not to substitute for them" (1992, 49).

Another important dimension of Noddings's vision is that each child will receive a unique education: there will be no unbending requirements, no mandatory courses, no monolithic body of knowledge that must be mastered. Children have different talents, interests, needs and goals, and should be educated accordingly. Teachers responding to Noddings's challenge to care need to have different, individualized expectations for each of their students.

Martin and Noddings have attempted to move from the global features of feminist thinking to the specific realities of classroom life. But their visions are different, reflecting the multiplicity of feminisms and the rich and multifaceted nature of schooling. I, too, intend to explore a vision of schooling, specifically early childhood education, that is rooted in feminism's emphasis on caring and connection and fueled by passion.

Little empirical research has been done on this topic. This is not surprising. As Mem Fox has said:

> Matters affecting the heart are far more elusive than those affecting the mind. There's no simple way to measure the role of the heart in teaching children . . . . It can't be recorded in numbers. It can't be caught in a statistical net. It can't be pre-tested or post-tested. Its subjects can't be divided into control groups because the affective aspects of any given situation are unique to the situation at the moment of its happening and cannot be replicated. Measuring such indefinables as the effects of expectations, happiness, eagerness, fondness, laughter, admiration, hope, humiliation, abuse, tiredness, racism, hunger, loneliness, and love on the development of literacy is so difficult, even within ethnographic research, that to my knowledge it is attempted rarely.
>
> But the affective won't go away. It's always there, whether researchers admit it or not. The plain old fact of the matter is that teachers and children have hearts, and those hearts play an enormous part in the teaching/learning process. (1995, 3–4)

The affective won't go away. And I certainly wouldn't want it to. But rather than ignore it—as other researchers have—I intend to focus upon it.

## Research design and methodology

I engaged in this research project in a primary grade classroom in the Loma Prieta Unified School District. The classroom of my teacher-partner, Martha George, gives life to the philosophies and practices that I associate with loving education. Martha is an experienced early childhood and elementary educator. She holds a B.A. degree in child development and an M.A. in curriculum and teacher education. She has been teaching for ten years, and has worked with children from birth through second grade. I feel privileged to have had the opportunity to work with such a gifted teacher.

In the fall of 1994, while this study was under way, Martha was teaching an ungraded primary class composed of nine kindergartners, seven first graders, and eight second graders. This was her first experience with this type of instructional arrangement, and her first time teaching second grade. Because I have several years' experience teaching second grade in the Loma Prieta school district, I felt that my presence as a collaborator in her classroom was able to make a meaningful contribution to her professional life and, hopefully, to the educational experiences of her students.

This study has a symmetrical design, following the shape of a bell curve. I began my stint in this classroom as a participant observer, spending approximately four weeks concentrating on the role of love in my teacher-partner's practice. I attempted to flesh out my notions of loving education during this phase of the research, focusing specifically on love's contribution to recurring structures of classroom life, such as circle times, classroom management, and transitions between activities. Though I attended to all aspects of Martha's classroom, I was particularly intrigued by the aspects of classroom life that are routine, taken for granted, unreflected-upon. Despite their somewhat anonymous nature, they are part of the implicit curriculum (Eisner 1985), and therefore have a powerful impact on children's experiences in school and on the ethos of the educational environment.

The study continued with an intensification of my teaching role, as I moved from the position of participant observer to participant contributor. During this phase of the research Martha and I shared responsibility for the life of the classroom—designing curricula, planning lessons, assessing student performance, organizing and managing classroom activities, and, of course, teaching—for the two-hour block of time I spent in her classroom each day. The specific content and parameters of this unit were developed in response to the needs and interests of Martha and her students: we created an interdisciplinary unit on family which drew on the California Language Arts (1987) and History–Social Science (1988) curriculum frameworks. The purpose of this four week phase of the research was to allow me to operationalize my theories about loving education and to reflect upon my own experiences as a loving teacher.

As the study drew to a close, I gradually shifted back to being a participant observer once again, phasing myself out of active contribution to classroom life over a three week period. This phasing-out served two purposes: First, it allowed me the opportunity to reexamine my initial impressions of Martha's practices and to further refine my vision of loving education as informed both by my observations of Martha and by my own teaching experiences in her classroom. Second, my stepping from the foreground into the background of classroom life made my departure seem less abrupt, less intrusive.

The data I gathered during this extended teaching and research collaboration fell into one of three strands: (1) information on the role of love in Martha's work, later crafted into a case study included here as Chapter Two; (2) information on the role of love in my own teaching practice, which I conceived of as a professional autobiography or as a self-study and which appears here as Chapter Three; and (3) information on the role of love in our teaching partnership, called the relational study, which is described in depth in Chapter Five. I did not approach each of these strands as a separate research endeavor to be completed in a linear fashion, one after the other. Because they are inextricably interwoven, I attended to all three strands throughout my time in the classroom, allowing each to develop naturally out of my experiences there. In my consideration of each strand, I used Sternberg's (1988a) definition of love—the interplay of intimacy, commitment, and passion—to guide and focus my observations.

I was a daily participant in the life of Martha's classroom for two hours each morning (from the opening of the school day until morning recess) from early October until the start of winter break in December. I deliberately chose to focus on a particular period of the school day, rather than a specific disciplinary area, at Martha's suggestion. Because she strongly advocates interdisciplinary teaching, teasing out one or two subjects for study in isolation seemed artificial and unhelpful to her, and directly contradicted the philosophical framework of her classroom. By focusing on a chunk of time that occurs naturally in the school day, I avoided that problem, and was able to engage in the disciplinary fullness of classroom life. Further, by arriving with the students and departing at a natural break in their daily routine, my presence in the classroom was better integrated and less obtrusive.

As the study began, I eased myself into classroom life. I started out on a chair at the side of the room, notebook in hand, and quickly ended up in the thick of things. During this period my participation was limited to sitting in class meetings, helping out at an activity station each day, and giving support to the children as they worked. I got to know the children, learned the rhythms of the classroom, and watched Martha in action. In the first week I took notes in a small notebook, but as I became more involved in classroom life, I found that note-taking interfered with my ability to work with the children. From that point on my reflections and observations were confined to my daily journal; in it I recorded the bulk of my data, writing daily following my time in the classroom. When the children had gone out for recess, Martha and I would spend time talking and reflecting on the morning. I would then sit at a computer in Martha's classroom and write up my observations. The writing time was built into the structure of my day; data collection continued in the same way throughout the co-teaching phase, and in the final participant observation period as well.

My daily journal entries were devoted principally to descriptions of the activities made available to the children during activity time, observations of the children's responses to and experiences with those activities, reflections on my own participation in the activities, description of Martha's role(s) each day, and preliminary explanations and analyses of what I was seeing and experiencing. I looked for examples of intimacy, commitment, and passion in the classroom, recording specific anecdotes where appropriate.

Each weekend I would reread the week's journal entries and write my "weekend reflections": asking myself questions, making notes of things to talk about with Martha, making tentative attempts to understand what I was experiencing in Martha's classroom. In other words, I wrote analytic memos to myself, or "notes-on-notes" (Kleinmann and Copp 1993), simultaneously collecting and analyzing my data.

Striving to keep the relationship between myself and Martha as collaborative as possible, I eschewed the standard data-gathering interview format in favor of more conversational interactions, as we engaged in daily debriefing-style informal discussions throughout the period during which I participated in her classroom. I would obtain specific and concrete information about classroom activities, receive clarification about particular details or intentions, and provide Martha with any feedback she might desire. Our relationship developed into a full-fledged teaching partnership, and these conversations grew to include curriculum deliberations, lesson planning, discussions of student work, and the like. They also became opportunities for Martha to give me feedback on my own teaching, thus providing a source of triangulation for my self-study strand.

Martha and I also had several longer and more structured conversations during the fieldwork period, in order to go into greater depth than was possible during the hustle and bustle of recess. Though there were certain topics I wanted to cover—and certain topics Martha wanted to cover—each conversation was less an interview than an "open-ended, negotiable situation" (Ayers 1989, 9). Topics included education (formal and informal; pre-K–12, college and professional training), family history, educational philosophy and practices, and reflections on the students in the class. The conversations were audiotaped, transcribed, and analyzed for incorporation into the finished narratives.

In addition to the conversations, Martha and I used a dialogue journal to exchange thoughts, questions, and information about our educational histories, philosophies, and experiences, and to explore specific topics related to the life of our classroom. Dialogue journals—usually a notebook shared by a pair of inquirers—are a common feature both in early childhood classrooms (Routman 1988) and in feminism-informed classrooms (see Brookes and Kelly 1989 for an example). The nature of the writings in such journals varies depending on the circumstances. In general, entries are not meant to be thoughtful or well-crafted essays, but rather gut-level and immediate responses to particular experiences, situations, or prompts. Martha and I both created prompts for each other, striving to make this a true dialogue, rather than a series of monologues. We also felt free to respond to each other's writings or to introduce topics of our own. Our writings provided opportunities for us to reflect on our teaching practices and on the beliefs that inform them. The technique also proved helpful in allowing us to "speak" safely and easily about topics that would have been difficult to grapple with face to face.

Data were also gathered through an interpretive art activity. Some people—Martha George (by her own admission) being one of them—are just not writers: music and the visual arts and dance exist to allow these people to express their thoughts and feelings. Furthermore, some things simply cannot be communicated through the written word (Eisner 1982). In asking Martha to write about her life in dialogue journals, I closed down certain avenues of expression, privileging some types of thoughts and disallowing others. To avoid this problem in his work with preschool teachers, Bill Ayers (1989) used interpretive activities that covered the same ground as interviews but led to different outcomes. He gave teachers clay and asked them to express or represent a significant event or theme in their work. In my version of this activity, Martha and I worked side by side, sculpting our clay and talking as we created. The conversation that ensued was of value to my research agenda, as were the finished artworks. Again, as in the case of the conversations and the dialogue journals, I was a full participant in this activity. The resulting data, our sculptures and our conversations, were analyzed three times: for insights they might yield into Martha's teaching, into my own practice, and into the relational nature of the experience of team-teaching in a loving classroom.

I analyzed and interpreted all of my data as an ongoing part of my data-gathering practices, attempting on a daily basis to make sense of what I had seen and experienced. In writing my analytic memos, I often found myself confronting interesting dilemmas and questions. The dialogue journal and daily debriefing enabled me to turn these around and discuss them with Martha immediately. Her feedback, opinions, ideas, and responses were woven into my data. Then, when my period of participation was complete, I made my first drafts available to her and encouraged her to respond to my interpretations of her teaching, my teaching, and our teaching relationship. I felt that it was extremely important to allow her feedback to become part of the public and finished work. Surprisingly, Martha did not agree. She was willing to give me off-the-record feedback, but felt that the chapters should stand as I wrote them. I have respected her wishes.

Finally, I did not code any of my data. Coding seemed a violent thing to do; and I did not feel that much would be gained from splintering my experience into tiny shards—it seemed that too much would be lost. I decided instead to try to think holistically about the data, focusing on complex themes and processes (Kleinmann and Copp 1993), a method that seemed consistent with my desired outcome as I hoped my narratives would be interesting to teachers as well as educational researchers. Susan Florio-Ruane recounts a troubling tale of research that fell short of that goal:

> Several years ago, after extended fieldwork in two classrooms, my research colleagues and I withdrew to the university to theorize and write about problems of writing instruction. Emerging nearly a year later, the researchers held in one hand a two-hundred page technical report titled "Schooling and the Acquisition of Written Literacy," and in the other, a five-paged Xeroxed report called "Findings of Practical Significance." The researchers stared at these two documents and wondered why their close and careful research had yielded so few findings of interest to teachers. (1986, 3)

Florio-Ruane and her colleagues found that their reports were received politely but without enthusiasm: they were not embraced even by those teachers whose realities they aimed to describe (1986, 5). I knew that my study was unlikely to make the best-seller list. But I did want it to have implications for practice, to be useful for teachers interested in love's role in the education of young children. As a piece of feminist work, it had a transformative agenda: I had undertaken this research to make a difference.

Though I was not sure how I would get there, I had known from the start of the project what I wanted my data chapters to look like. I knew I wanted to write an account only an educational researcher could write; but I also wanted to write an account that only a *teacher* could write, to create narratives that would capture the heart and the soul of our professional experience. I wanted humor. I wanted life. I wanted children to be present in the text. I wanted to write narratives that teachers and parents of young children could read, and might even *want* to read, data stories as compelling and as vibrant as classroom life itself. And I wanted my data stories to be as good as Martha's teaching.

# 2
## Living Loving Teaching

Open the door to Room 4 at Bayview Elementary School, and the first thing you see is a small sign that reads, "Opening the classroom door should be as exciting as opening a gift package." Martha George's classroom fulfills this promise and offers more besides. The room is bursting with color, activity, with the humming noise of busy, engaged thinkers at work. Every inch of wall space is covered with student work, with poetry, with mathematics problems, with books, with art. The chalkboards are plastered over with charts, song lyrics, life-sized "wild thing" costumes. Moons and stars hang from the ceiling, paper chains in brightly colored repeating patterns dangle from the edges of the loft. The shelves are brimming with games, puzzles, and blocks, the counter tops crowded with piles of student work in progress—outer space dictionaries, lanterns, decoupaged boxes, stargazers. Public library books, school library books, classroom library books, books written by individual students and by the class as a whole overflow their tubs, bins, and chalkboard ledges and flood out onto the rug in the meeting area.

A handful of children are in the back of the room building Lego™ rockets and spacecrafts to land on the relief map of the moon's surface that they made yesterday. Others are playing with play-dough that is as black as outer space itself. Another group of children is bending over a creative writing project, conversing quietly and discussing questions of spelling. Beside them is a boisterous group of "landlords" evicting "tenants" made of base ten blocks from overcrowded "apartments" in a game that introduces the mathematical concept of place value. Two girls are reading on the sofa. A pair of feet in muddy Power Ranger sneakers peek out from under a pile of cushions in the reading area under the loft: listen closely and hear the sound of an emergent reader making his way through a book about Clifford the Big Red Dog. In the loft above him, a family is busily making dinner in the house area—pots are being stirred by a girl in a wedding dress and sunglasses, and a boy in a hat talks on the phone he's tucked between his ear and his shoulder as he rocks his baby.

Try to find Martha. She's a small, slight woman in her early thirties, not much bigger than some of the second graders. Her ponytail, jeans, and Keds sneakers add to her camouflage—she blends in with the children in her class as she sits among them at the work tables in the room. Though the room is noisy, she rarely raises her voice: she speaks quietly to a child or to a small group of children rather than attempting to address the class as a whole. That strategy works well in this particular learning environment: it is a multi-age kindergarten, first, and second grade class, in which the students' range of abilities, attention spans, interests, and maturity levels is vast.

Martha walks over and turns out the lights. It is ten o'clock. "Kids may stop what they are doing and get their snacks and go outside for recess. If you're painting, please finish up and wash your hands before you leave." Though they were deep in concentration moments before the lights went out, the children drop everything and stampede out of the classroom doors.

Bayview Elementary School is an alternative school in the Loma Prieta Unified School District which is located in an affluent Northern California suburb. Rather than drawing its student population from the surrounding neighborhood, as most schools in the district do, Bayview enrolls students from throughout the entire district. Founded in 1971 in response to burgeoning interest in open education, Bayview remains an open school today, characterized by, in the words of its principal Alexander Ganz, "open doors, open policies, and open relationships" (Darling 1994, 20). Alexander describes Bayview's mission in the *1993–4 Report to the Community:*

> We are committed to providing ongoing opportunities for all children to build strong self-concepts, develop positive and productive human relationships, and foster a lifelong love of learning. In order to meet the academic, emotional, physical, and social needs of our students, we continually strive to maintain a balance between the content and processes of learning, between intellectual and experiential education, and between the needs of the group and the needs of the individual. Because we believe equally in caring for each other and caring for our environment, teaching and learning at Bayview are characterized by activities that are developmentally appropriate, child-centered, and

designed—through collaboration and cooperation—to enhance children's perspectives and establish ties to the world in which we live. (2)

Parents who are interested in helping their children obtain this type of education enter their names in a lottery and hope to be admitted: there were two applicants for each of the thirty-three kindergarten slots available for the 1997–1998 school year.

The atmosphere at Bayview is very informal. Students call teachers and administrators by their first names. There are no bells to signal the start or close of the day. Student work is evaluated without letter grades. All of the classes comprise more than one grade level: most of the classes combine two grades, and several combine three. The purpose of all these innovations is to enable children to learn in an environment that is flexible, process-oriented, challenging, and stimulating. An important part of the Bayview philosophy is the expectation that children will take responsibility for themselves, their behavior and their learning, and will make as many of their own choices and decisions as they can.

At the start of her tenth year of teaching, Martha George chose to come to Bayview to teach an ungraded primary class. She had been teaching in the Loma Prieta Unified School District for a year, and had been very comfortable and happy in her kindergarten at Tatum Elementary School, but teaching an ungraded primary class had long been an aspiration. Bayview had successfully piloted the idea of a K-1-2 classroom, was looking to add a second one, and they were also about to pilot an ungraded 3-4-5 classroom. This was the opportunity of a career.

The term "ungraded" does not mean the elimination of assessment and evaluation of student work, but the elimination of the age-graded structure common to most educational environments in this country. Ungraded classrooms (sometimes referred to as nongraded classrooms, mixed age or multi-age groupings) acknowledge that "the realities of child development defy the rigorous ordering of children's abilities and attainments into conventional graded structure" (Goodlad and Anderson 1959, 3). Martha's class, for example, is composed of twenty-four children who would be labelled kindergartners (five boys and four girls in this case), first graders (three boys and four girls) or second graders (three boys, five girls) in a more conventional setting. In Room 4 they are referred to—with a deliberate lack of specificity—as "olders" and "youngers." There is no attempt to teach separate curricula to the children from each grade. All of the academic activities are made available to all students, and performance expectations are fluid, based generally on ability, not chronological age. Ungraded classrooms like Martha's deal honestly with the vicissitudes of child development, allowing children to learn and grow at their own pace.

Bayview has favored multi-age classrooms since its inception as an alternative school. Apart from the two K-1-2 classes and the new 3-4-5, the combination classes span only two grade levels. They exist as a result of the school's ideological and philosophical orientation. Multi-age groupings give children the opportunity to be both a younger and an older in the same classroom; they provide opportunities for cross-age tutoring; and they are developmentally appropriate, fostering flexibility and responsiveness to the individual needs of the particular students. Combination classes are becoming increasingly common at other schools in the district. though, in most cases these classes arise out of convenience and a desire to reduce class size, rather than from a deeply held philosophical commitment.

Martha's own interest in multi-age classes began during her undergraduate years. She majored in child development, only deciding to pursue a teaching credential as an afterthought:

> My advisor gave me some information about the fact that you could get a teaching credential without going through an education program. (I really wasn't interested in doing that, because I had grown up pretty much next to Fitchburg State College, which was a teacher's college, and I was NOT interested in going to a "teacher's college" and doing that whole route. I did not want to do that.) But so, my big focus in being at college was not to become a teacher. I thought "Well, I could take these few extra classes, do student teaching, and I'll have a credential as well as a developmental psychology degree."

Martha did her student teaching in an alternative school in Cambridge, Massachusetts, a school very much like Bayview—multi-age classes, children staying with the same teacher for several years, curricula developed by the teachers—and forged her vision of what schooling should be like.

After graduation, Martha opted to work in day care rather than in a public school setting. She worked at The Capitol Harbor Children's Center (affectionately known as "Kiddie City"), a child care facility in Cambridge, Massachusetts, with a philosophy closely aligned to her own. She team-taught with a woman who had never been trained as a teacher but who, as Martha says, "was just one of the most incredible teachers I've ever seen. In some ways it was probably best that she hadn't been trained as a teacher because she just didn't have any boundaries on what she was willing to try and to do with the kids." Martha recalled a typical Kiddie City experience:

> We had days that were entirely paint days, and the kids would go from one paint station to another and try painting. We made these helmets with paintbrushes on them so that you could paint with your head, we had feet painting— we had these big trays and we had these rails on the walls, and the kids would stand on the tray and hang on to the rails and slide their feet around and paint with their feet. I guess there were no limits. We were really left to be as creative as we wanted when it came to what activities we thought would be valuable and interesting to kids.

When Martha graduated from college, she felt unprepared to be a public school teacher: too young, too tentative, too inexperienced. But she says, "I became a teacher at Kiddie City," and after several years there she felt ready to go out on her own professionally. She left Massachusetts for a public school teaching job in San Andreas, California; she then moved on to the Loma Prieta Unified School District, some fifteen miles south of her previous school. Martha had been at Bayview one month, teaching her ungraded primary class, when I joined her in her classroom.

❖ ❖ ❖ ❖ ❖ ❖

Martha arrives at school long before her students, readying her classroom while the morning sky is still dark. Though it starts with just a trickle, a steady stream of minivans and Volvo station wagons soon fills the parking lot, and the sounds of children fill the air. There are no bells to wait for: Martha's students kiss their moms or dads goodbye and charge straight into their classroom, dragging their backpacks, lunch boxes, and other accoutrements of childhood. They all seem to know just what to do, unpacking their belongings, turning over their attendance cards, and putting lunch tickets into a special cannister. The children do not have individual desks, as they might in some elementary school classrooms, so special treasures—little hair barrettes, baseball cards, geodes, plastic doodads of all kinds— are secreted away in cubbies to be retrieved at recess.

Martha perches on a tiny child-size chair on the open patch of carpet at the side of the room. She talks and jokes with the children who gather around her. Several children lie on the rug reading books, others sit on the unsightly brown plaid sofa. Every so often Martha breaks away from her conversation to redirect a child who has gotten too boisterous: "Connor, do you remember what you are supposed to be doing right now?" she asks gently.

She begins each day the same way, with meeting. "Okay! Please put your books away and come over to the rug to hear the lunch choices," she says. Even the children who are not buying lunch come over excitedly: they know that listening carefully to the lunch count will pay off. Martha continues, "The choices for today are baked chicken, wild pizza, sub sandwich, nachos, or hamburger." Martha stops what she is doing and turns to look at a wiggling, giggling boy with shiny black hair. "Andy . . ." she says quietly. Andy is busy poking at the boy sitting beside him, unaware that he is the focus of the teacher's attention. Martha tries again, a bit louder this time. "Andy." He looks up at her sheepishly and puts his hands in his lap. "Andy, you're going to want to listen carefully to this so that you can make a good decision about lunch." Martha does not scold or reprimand. Andy simply needs to listen so that he can make a good choice. The message is clear: the behavior itself is not bad, but it prevents Andy from taking responsibility for himself, and that's a problem. Martha continues the lunch count, marking the children's choices on the attendance clipboard.

The lunch count is then transformed into the math problem of the day: "One person ordered chicken, three people ordered pizza, zero people ordered the submarine sandwich, two people ordered nachos, and one person ordered a hamburger. How many lunches is that all together?" Martha asks the class. As she reads off the tally, the children count on their fingers, keeping track of the total. "If you think you have the answer, hold up that number of fingers and show it to a friend," Martha says. The children wave their hands wildly, fingers outstretched. Most hold up seven, a few hold eight or six. Some of the youngers look around quickly and put up the same number of fingers as their neighbor;

others simply put both hands in the air and wiggle all of their fingers. Martha continues the routine. "When I count to three you can call out your answer. 1 . . . 2 . . . 3!" The room echoes with the sound of children joyfully calling out "SEVEN!!!" "Oh, I heard a lot of sevens, that's great," concludes Martha. The children squirm with joy and pull down their clenched fists, hissing "yesssss!" as if they had just hit the lottery jackpot. Even those children who yelled out "SIX" or "EIGHT" are excited—they had meant to say seven, after all! The children love the math problem of the day, not even realizing how masterfully Martha has turned a mundane, content-free time into a lesson in mental mathematics rooted in a practical, real-world problem.

Meeting continues. Gus, a very small boy with translucent white skin who is clearly "a younger," raises his hand and calls out, "Martha? Connor is bothering me . . . ." He looks indignant, clearly The Wronged Party, and waits smugly for Martha to have a few words with Connor. Martha looks at Gus and whispers her response as she gropes for the orange marker beneath her chair. "Do you know who you need to talk to about that?" she asks. Gus seems unsure, and thinks for a moment, brow furrowed. It is likely that in his previous school experiences, or at playdates, or in the park, an adult has been summoned to settle disputes and smooth ruffled feathers. "A grown-up?" he suggests. Martha shakes her head and replies, "I think that you can talk to Connor about that." Again, Martha shifts the locus of responsibility back onto the students. They need to solve their own problems, make their own choices, and learn to take responsibility for their own behavior.

As Martha steps over to the calendar, she asks Mitchell to move away from Mark. She issues her request in a whisper, as if misbehavers do not deserve her full voice. Like the lunch count, the calendar routine is suffused with mathematical concepts: odd and even numbers, patterning, place value, graphing. Mitchell does not move and continues to bother Mark and some of the other children around him. Martha whirls around, marker poised in midair. She gives Mitchell a stern look, and says firmly, "Mitchell, if you want to choose a new spot for yourself, you will have to do it now. If you don't, I'll choose for you." Mitchell wants to choose for himself; he wants to make a good decision. He stands, moves away from Mark, and finds a new spot, turning around like a puppy several times before sitting down.

Martha finishes the calendar and returns to her little chair. She picks up a book, puts it in her lap and raises both her fists in the air. She opens her mouth to speak, and a child interrupts. "Let's count in Spanish," Sophie says. "We did Spanish yesterday, didn't we?" replies Martha. Another voice chimes in, "No, let's count by twos!" "Fours! Fours! Fours!" calls another. "Ummmm . . . Let's count by tens today," Martha decides. The children know just what to do. They raise their fists and the counting begins, with one finger raised up for each number. Slowly the begin to chant: "10, 20, 30, 40, 50, 60, 70, 80, 90, 100!" They take a deep breath, exhale noisily, and recite a poem:

> Tiddle dee tiddle dee beet beet!
> A book is fun to eat, eat!
> No, it's not! No, it's not!
> A book is fun to READ.

Martha clearly knows the value of routine. Bayview may have a reputation for being unstructured and chaotic, but Martha's classroom is just the opposite. She has created an environment in which young children are able to take responsibility for themselves because they know just what is expected and how things work. She has built a framework, a skeleton, sturdy and strong, which the children flesh out with their good decisions.

The children have just reminded themselves that a book is fun to read, and all eyes are on Martha—even Mitchell's, Andy's, Connor's, and Gus's. They are ready. Martha reads the class a story that is linked to the unit they have been doing on space and the solar system, then describes the activities for the day. The remainder of the morning will be devoted to activity time.

Martha plans five different activities for each day, all of which go on simultaneously at different locations in the classroom. On any given day there is an assortment of adults in the room—Martha's aide Yvette, a variety of tutors employed by the district, parent volunteers—and each activity is generally supervised by an adult. Once the children have finished their work they are welcome to read, write in their journals, work on ongoing mathematics projects, or have free choice, which includes playing with blocks, Legos™, or puzzles, doing small scale art projects, playing in the house area, or working with clay.

Martha describes each of the activities to the children during meeting. In the case of art projects she will often produce an example right there on the rug, elaborating on the techniques she is using: "When I am cutting out this shape, I move the paper as I cut. I don't twist my scissor hand all around, I move the paper. See?"

When activity time begins, the children go to stations that Martha has selected for them. These placements are made very deliberately, as Martha pays such close attention to the children as individuals. This close attention, and the sensitivity that characterizes her decision making, are evidence that the seeds of intimacy Martha planted in September are beginning to take root. Martha explains:

> It depends on what [activities] I've got out and who I think will work together well or not. And sometimes it's more because I've seen certain kids have an interest in each other and I'll pair them together. Sometimes I try to structure it so that there's a real heterogeneous group of ability in terms of kids who will be able to help each other, kids who are going to need support functioning at that station. And I also try to somewhat balance it for boys and girls . . . . Sometimes they fall out that way—certain activities attract more boys to them or more girls to them. I try to encourage kids who I think would not try certain things . . . to try everything, to go everywhere.

The children sitting on the rug at Martha's feet do not know about how carefully their needs, personalities, and desires are taken into consideration when these decisions are made. They just know that Martha has a tiny square of paper with the class list printed on it that tells who goes where, and that almost every morning meeting ends with Martha searching for her misplaced list. She finds it quickly this morning, and the children lean forward, eager to hear where they will be sent. Some even have their fingers crossed for good luck, hoping to be sent to the activity of their choice.

"At the round table," Martha says, pointing, "kids will be working on making their solar system puzzles. They need to be colored, glued, and then cut, just like I showed you. It needs to happen in that order, or else it will get very tricky." She reads the names of the children going to that station. Someone groans. Either he is disappointed to be sent to this activity when he wanted to do another, or he is disappointed not to be chosen to do this activity first. The reason isn't clear, but the emotion is. Elementary school can be a world ruled by fear of scarcity and craving for fairness, and clearly someone is worried. Martha looks up from the list, eyebrow cocked. "Will you get to do all of the activities?" she asks the class. No one answers. "Will everyone get to do all of the activities?" she asks again. "Yes!" they reply in unison. Though it is early in the school year, intimacy has been growing, and they trust her.

"At the zigzag table," Martha continues, "Moon reports. Olders need to look in the books on the table and find three facts about the moon that you would like to include in your report. Youngers may pick up one of the sheets that I made and trace the words." She reads off the names, but does not specify who is an older and who is a younger. Second graders are olders, kindergartners are youngers, for certain. But where do the first graders fit? I asked Martha about this, and she replied:

> It depends. It is not cut and dried at all and it varies from situation to situation. I usually leave it up to the kids to decide. Well, that's not entirely true either. I expect the second graders to do the more demanding option, and they know that. And I assume that most of the kinders will choose the simpler option. Though sometimes they surprise me, like Brian or Robert will choose to do the olders' page. And that's fine. The first graders tend to . . . well, some of the first graders, like Lauren or Eleanor are very capable academically, and they'll always opt to do the harder page. And some of the first graders who are just getting started with their writing skills, like Li Ping, for example, will take the easier page, and that's okay. And there are some first graders who are capable but who don't want to put forth much effort . . . they do the easier page too. And though that is not what I'd want for them academically, it tells me something about where they are at in other areas of their development. Sometimes I'll push those kids, and sometimes I won't. It depends.

Martha's approach to teaching is rooted in a commitment to each child as an individual. As she wrote in our dialogue journal: "It is very important to me that I respond to each child as an individual, which means really knowing them, which means investing in them emotionally." Responding to children as individuals is one of the fundamental tenets of both progressive education and high quality early childhood education. However, Martha takes this one step further. She is not content to stop at "really knowing them" in order to respond to their individual needs: she sees "investing in them emotionally" as necessary also. This emotional investment, a manifestation of Sternberg's (1988a) intimacy component of love, is one way that love plays a role in Martha's life as a teacher. She not only thinks carefully about each child, but also cares deeply about each child, and about each child's experience in the classroom.

In addition to evoking Sternberg, this aspect of Martha's professional practice is related to feminist moral theory. In her work on maternal thinking, Sara Ruddick (1989) describes how mothers' thinking begins with careful devotion to a specific and particular child or set of children, i.e., their own; thus maternal thinking is a phenomenon rooted in experience and located within the family, which then can radiate outwards. Like maternal thinking, Martha's teacherly thinking also seems rooted in experience. She focuses tightly on the particular needs, concerns, strengths, and weaknesses of each child in her class, and then makes her professional decisions accordingly. As Martha pointed out, teaching in this manner requires a great deal of emotional investment. This is in direct contrast to Lilian Katz's assertions, described in Chapter One, that teachers should be impartial and approach their interactions with their children with an air of "detached concern" (Katz 1981, 15), rather than with deep feelings of attachment and caring.

Love also plays a role in Martha's lesson planning. As she wrote in our dialogue journal:

> This is not something I think about explicitly for every activity I choose, but I think that love guides my overall choices. I mean, I want activities that the kids will love and remember, activities that will stretch them to find out something not just about the activities but about themselves as well. More specifically, love influences my decisions because I connect what I know about each child as an individual with what activities they would particularly connect with or enjoy. I think about who will be really good at an activity and gain emotionally from that and/or share their success with the others.

Martha focuses on the needs, strengths, and desires of the children, and she plans their educational experiences in a way that will lead not only to increased knowledge but also to emotional growth.

In this quote, Martha uses the word love in two different ways. Though she does not think about it explicitly for every activity she designs or selects, Martha acknowledges that her love for the children "guides [her] overall choices." She states "love influences my decisions because I connect what I know about each child as an individual with what activities they would particularly connect with or enjoy": she feels that love informs her practices, plays a role in her curricular decision making. It is love for her students that motivates her to select particular lessons or activities. Though she does not say so directly in this passage, it is also clear that Martha wants the children to love the activities that she has chosen for them. Love is working on two levels here: love between teacher and students and love between students and educational experiences.

As the solar system puzzle makers and moon report writers leave the meeting area, Martha dismisses the other children to their stations. Some will be making samples of Mars soil with sand, steel wool, and water. Some will be writing in their journals about the Mars lander spacecrafts that they built during activity time yesterday. The rest will be doing a complicated activity with pattern blocks: they will build a pattern of their own design using the same number of blocks as they are years old, then recreate this pattern exactly using paper shapes, and finally glue their shapes onto a square of paper. Martha has told the children that the squares will soon be connected together into a class quilt.

Martha's plans for the pattern block activity reflect her desire that each lesson work on several different levels of sophistication and complexity. This is important in all classrooms, but it is imperative in a multi-age group. Though olders and youngers work side by side on the same activity, their experiences will be very different. Using age as the guideline for the number of blocks included in each design cleverly ensures that the youngers will have simpler designs. As they do this math lesson, the children also practice their fine motor skills as they build, arrange, and glue. Children are able to work to the level of their own ability and take from this activity whatever they need.

The room is a busy place as the children work. Once they finish one activity they are free to move on to another. This rotation through all the stations around the room is left almost entirely to the children. No timers ding, no buzzers sound to force the children to move on to the next activity. Martha values self-direction, and trusts the children to make good choices: they move to their next activity when they are ready, and select whichever appeals to them most. Before I saw it I found this hard to imagine—so I did a lot of watching.

Lauren finished her Mars soil sample, washed her hands, and headed for the zigzag table and the moon reports. But there were no seats left at the zigzag table: that activity station was full. Lauren stopped behind Catherine's chair, hand on her slender hip and head tilted to one side, with her long blond ponytail still swinging. She looked around the room. There was space at the solar system puzzle table; there was space at the pattern blocks table, but she had already been there. The journal table was almost empty: Travis was there, with his head resting on his outstretched arm, a blank piece of paper in front of him. I could almost hear Lauren thinking, "Hmmm. Solar system puzzles or journal writing . . . ?" She wrinkled up her nose. She wanted to do her moon report, but there was no space left at that station. Then suddenly her face lit up, and she reached over for a few of the nonfiction books that were resting unused on the table as some of the youngers traced their reports. She grabbed a clipboard, took the books and her blank report sheet, and sat down on the rug in the meeting area. In a few minutes she was immersed in her work, a six-year-old astronomer pondering the mysteries of the universe.

Of course, it doesn't always work so smoothly. Martha looks up from Li Ping's moon report, interrupted by Carlos whizzing by behind her chair shouting, "Brian! Brian! I'm Superman!" Martha walks over to Carlos, bends down and puts her arm around his shoulders. "Carlos, have you done your Mars soil yet?" she asks. Carlos nods. "And you already did your moon report. Okay, good. Can I see your solar system puzzle?" Carlos looks at her blankly. "Did you color and glue and cut your puzzle, Carlos?" Martha asks. With her arm still around him, Martha guides Carlos over to the round table and gives him his page and a pair of scissors. "Have fun, Superman," she says as she walks back to the moon report table. Martha sees that Li Ping is working fine without her help. So she continues on, surveying the room. Travis is still at the journal table, where he has been for the past twenty minutes. He is staring into space now, leaning way back in his chair. The page before him is blank. On her way to the journal table Martha stops to show Amy how to work the Elmer's glue bottle: "See how this bottle has an orange head and no neck? To make the glue come out you need to twist the head so he has a neck. See?"

The room feels a bit like Grand Central Station at rush hour. It is noisy. It hums with activity. The children move around, bumping and jostling each other, determined to get where they are going. They are focused on their goals, their destinations. But Martha would not have it any other way. "It's hard," she says. "But you know (pause) the alternative of having everybody doing the same thing (pause) it doesn't really feel comfortable to me." The reasons for her discomfort reflect her deep commitment to the children as unique individuals. First, having a five-ring circus enables her to put out a variety of activities that cover different academic areas—writing, mathematics, art—and different types of learning modalities—aural, kinesthetic, visual. Research (e.g., Gardner 1983) indicates that schools tend to focus only on the development of language and mathematical skills and capabilities, ignoring other kinds of intelligence. This is not the case in Martha's classroom. There is something for everybody here, and everyone has a chance to work in the ways they like best.

The children also have the chance to work in the ways they like least, and to grow as a result. Eisner (1982) describes the crucial importance of providing access for all students to all modalities and all forms of information representation. Each form of representation is unique and exists for a specific reason: poetry says things that cannot be communicated through any other medium, as does mathematics, or dance. Exposure to all the different forms of representation develops different aspects of cognition. If children are never encouraged to write poetry, or to paint, or to sing, those forms of thinking will never be developed. This will limit the children's ability to experience the fullness of understanding. In a recent study, Singer (1991) found that high school students do not consider painting, film, music, or dance to be valid sources of historical information. By the time these children reached high school, then, their experiences in school had led them to conclude that text is the only legitimate source of information. Had the children in Singer's study been students in classrooms like Martha's, perhaps they would have had more exposure to the kinds of knowledge embedded in less conventional forms of representation, and would feel more comfortable with them.

Finally, Martha's classroom arrangement allows the children some flexibility. Martha says, "Not everybody is at the point to do everything the same at any given time, and so, while I send them off to their activities to start with, if somebody wasn't ready to be there, like Carlos really wasn't ready to do his Halloween book, fine, he could go and do cutting." Children are welcome to make their own decisions, to do what feels right to them. Martha affirms NAEYC's assertion that providing opportunities for the children to practice self-direction will enable the children to see themselves as competent and capable people (Bredekamp 1987).

Martha herself sees the children as competent and capable people, and she respects their interests, desires, and choices. She says:

> I just feel like having only one thing out (pause) it puts all of the weight on me to decide what that one thing is, and all of my values are invested in it (pause) of what I think is important. And I think that all of these activities are good activities, but I also know that the kids will sort them out and choose the ones that they value, and think are the most important. Some I choose to have everybody do, and some are literally choices.

Martha is willing to let go of the expectation that all of the children will complete all of the activities in order to give them the opportunity to be self-directed.

Allowing certain activities to be optional frees Martha from having to be a watchdog walking around the room with a clipboard, checking off children's names as they complete each activity. Sometimes she leaves a class list on each activity table and the children cross off their names as they finish; other times she sorts through completed work at the end of the day and makes notes about whose work is missing. This sorting also provides an opportunity for evaluation: record keeping is mainly done through anecdotal observations and informal assessment of student work.

Martha's commitment to allowing the children to be self-directed also provides opportunities for children to slip through the day without doing certain activities. This bothered the watchdog in me, but it does not upset Martha. She says: "There are other activities. So it's not that I feel like those kids (pause), because they don't do it at that time, they're never going to get that experience. There are plenty of other opportunities for that experience." Having the children remain in her classroom for more than one academic year gives Martha the confidence to know that all of the necessary experiences will happen at one time or another, and the freedom to shrug off some of the pressures of coverage that plague other teachers.

As activity time continues, Martha moves through the room constantly. I mapped her route through the room one morning, tracing her path from station to station, and ended up with a drawing that looked like an explosion in a spaghetti factory. As she moves, she redirects wanderers, settles down beside strugglers, celebrates successes, and prevents failures. She is everywhere at once. She moves back and forth, forth and back, whirling around as the children call her name. Martha! Martha! Martha! Martha! She sits on the floor, crouches alongside the tables, steps over chairs in a dance of teaching that is magnificent to watch.

And then it is 10:00. Recess comes and goes without much fanfare. The children leap up from their work, grab their snacks, and barrel out the door at the appointed time. When recess ends they run back in with equal gusto and pick up their work where they left off. Activity time continues for another hour. Most of the children get to finish everything. And if they don't there is always tomorrow: everyone gets a chance to do everything, just as Martha promised, and finishing yesterday's work is always an option.

The morning ends where it began, on the rug in the meeting area. The class reconvenes to hear the next installment of the chapter book that Martha has been reading aloud to them. Then it is time for lunch, and the end of the day for the kinders. In the afternoons the olders work on their math menus, have literature groups, and delve more deeply into content than they are able to do when the kinders are present. The day continues, but rush hour is over till tomorrow morning at 9:00.

❖❖❖❖❖❖

Their voices get louder and louder. A group of children is standing around a table, building lunar modules out of small white boxes and tin foil. As they work, Gus and Rita test each other's math knowledge. Gus starts it. "I know what ten plus ten plus ten is," he brags. "Big deal." replies Rita, "so does everybody.

It's thirty." Rita's words must have stung; Gus upped the ante. "Well, do you know what one hundred take away fifty is? Do you?" he asks, clearly assuming that she doesn't. "Duh!" Rita disdainfully says, not even dignifying his question with a response. "It's fifty," Gus tells her. "I knew that, Gus," Rita haughtily replies.

Gus is a kindergartner, Rita a second grader. The interaction I was witnessing seemed like a snippet of footage from one of those nature shows on public television in which the young bucks are sparring to determine status rankings in the herd. Gus didn't have a chance, but he clearly didn't know that.

The intensity of the interaction rises and falls. Sometimes it seems like a game, sometimes it seems like an argument.

". . . Eight! And what's seven plus nine?", asks Rita. "Who cares?" replies Gus. Rita laughs. "What's three plus four?" Gus asks her. "Seven, of course. What's one hundred take away three?" she asks. No answer. "What's one hundred take away three, Gus? Gus!" Rita says. She had hit the ball into his court and was waiting for it to come back. Gus was suddenly very busy with his lunar module. He didn't look up. "Well," I heard Rita say, "if you're not stupid, then answer!" Gus's face turns bright red, and he yells, "I'm not stupid! You're stupid!" Rita looks as if she had been slapped: a kindergartner has told her she is stupid. She composes herself quickly. "No, Gus," she explains in a calm and patronizing voice, "I'm not stupid. I know what one hundred take away three is. *You* are stupid."

Dara looks up from her lunar module. "This whole thing is stupid," she says. "Why don't you both be quiet and do your work?" Calm settles over the lunar module table, and the math war is forgotten. I found this interaction disturbing. That day I wrote in my journal:

> Though Martha seems to see everything, there is stuff she misses. A second grader was teasing a kinder about being stupid and not knowing anything. Does Martha know that this goes on? How does she handle it, deal with it? The older kid picking on Gus really upset me—me more than him, even. It bothers me the mom—I hate to see kids getting hurt and I hate to see kids being mean, and it bothers me the teacher—I tended to sit on and squelch this kind of thing—I monitored things much more closely than Martha seems to.
> (Field notes 11/10/94)

I assumed that Martha hadn't known that this was going on. Had she known about it, she would have put a stop to it, I thought. But when I asked her about it, I found that she had known exactly what was going on but had opted not to step in. I was surprised by her response:

> Gus is someone who (pause) provokes that kind of mean response. And so, to a certain extent, if he's going to set himself into that role and he's going to say "well, I know this and you don't," then, to a certain extent, I want him to have an understanding of what's going to happen if he's going to be making those kinds of assertions to other kids. Particularly with math, that's an area where Rita felt very frustrated and very poorly skilled last year, especially being a first in a 1-2 [a first/second grade combination class], that's something she's really longing to prove that she knows how to do. It's really important for her to feel successful in that area because I think she felt incredibly unsuccessful in that area last year, from all reports that I've heard.

An interaction that I had perceived as a random act of meanness actually had significant implications, given the specific realities of the children involved. Rita needed to feel successful, and Gus needed to learn more about the navigation of social situations. Rather than intervening with a blanket proclamation prohibiting meanness in the classroom, Martha evaluated the specific interaction in its broader context and held back, believing that the lessons learned would be greater than any hurt suffered. This kind of flexibility and responsiveness to the individual needs of the children is a hallmark of Martha's teaching.

Coupled with this flexibility is the ability to let go. Martha did not rush in to offer advice or to solve problems in this situation, or in many others like it that I witnessed during my time in Room 4. She will step in to redirect children whose behavior is impeding the work of others—people talking during meeting or loudly pretending to be Superman during work time. But when the children are having an interpersonal conflict, as Gus and Rita were at the lunar module table, Martha prefers to hang back and let the children solve their own problems.

Martha is willing to relinquish control of many aspects of classroom life that other teachers grasp tenaciously. She lets children make their own way through the day's activities, at their own pace and in their own sequence. Children may even skip a particular activity with no repercussions. They work together to solve their social problems. In Martha's vision of classroom life, the children need to take responsibility for themselves, make their own choices, fight their own battles. They will make mistakes. They will do things the hard way. And they will learn by doing.

Though Martha's classroom generally runs smoothly, late in October I had the opportunity to witness a difficult morning. Andy and Mitchell were poking each other with pencils at the Jupiter report table. Maria and Chihoe were wandering around aimlessly. Dara, Sophie, and Eleanor were play-fighting on the rug, their math assignments crumpled beneath their dirty white sneakers. But Martha ignored them, concentrating on her work with Peter. She is no policeman: her energies are best spent teaching, not disciplining, and the children need to learn to take responsibility for themselves.

Martha is a very unobtrusive presence in her own classroom. She is a soft-spoken and reserved person by nature, the kind of woman who would pass up the chance to be queen in favor of being the power behind the throne. When we were studying together in graduate school, one of our professors casually mentioned to me that he was pleased and surprised by the quality of her term paper, since she had not said much in class. He hadn't realized how bright she was, as she had not made an effort to show off for him as other students did. "She is very . . . inscrutable," he concluded. The professor was right, and the word "inscrutable" quickly became an inside joke for me and Martha.

Inscrutable or not, she does not refrain from communicating her loving feelings to her students. She said in our dialogue journal, "I think that many of the kids know I care by the way I act and know them. I try to communicate in lots of subtle ways— knowing about them, my interest in them, etc. . . . I'm not an emotionally flowery person, so I don't do lots of real big shows of affection. (You know me, I'm so inscrutable!)"

Her disinterest in "real big shows of affection" limits the amount of hugging in her classroom practice, but Martha does not avoid close physical contact with the children. Maria rests her head on Martha's knee during meeting one morning; Martha strokes her hair gently. Carlos cuts his finger; Martha pats his back reassuringly as he applies a Band-Aid to his wound. She might not initiate spontaneous hugs or cuddles like many primary teachers, but she always responds warmly to the children's advances.

She uses touch in other significant ways. Whenever a child comes over to Martha to read his work aloud, or whenever she crouches beside a working child to read his work, Martha puts her hand around his shoulder or on his back. This touch creates a bond between teacher and student, an island of calm amid the hubbub of the classroom. Martha's touch seems to suggest to the children that she really cares about their work and wants to give it her full attention. Interestingly, other children rarely attempt to interrupt these pairings: it is as if Martha's touch creates a boundary that needs to be respected.

When children need redirecting, like Andy and Mitchell with their poking pencils, or Dara, Eleanor, and Sophie tussling on the rug, Martha will get up from her work with another child rather than yelling across the room. And she intervenes with touch. She touches the children on the back, arm, or shoulder as she talks. Her touch seems to help them center themselves, and calms them down. She speaks softly to them, using only positive statements: "I can't let you put your whole body up on that table, Mitchell. It's not safe" or "Andy, do you know what you should be doing now?" and then, "Andy, you have two choices. You can get to work on your math or you can cut out your Jupiter. Which will it be?"—and then lets go, allowing the child to make a choice. No "stop." No "don't." No "no." She has developed a discipline strategy that draws both on her caring feelings for the children and her goal of helping them to make choices and take responsibility for themselves and their behavior. She maintains a consistently positive affect in her redirections. Martha meets misbehavior with tenderness and love.

Then, as suddenly as they arose, the difficulties dissolve. Andy and Mitchell get to work, and the girls on the rug disperse into other parts of the classroom. Maria is up in the house area now, planning her wedding to Gus. Only Chihoe remains, wandering around the room and pestering the children who are working. "I said cut it out, Chihoe!" someone snaps angrily. Martha looks up from her work with Kristen. She gets up and walks over to Chihoe. She bends down low and puts her hand on his back, saying, "Chihoe, it looks like you have a few minutes. Come and do some math with me." She takes his hand and they walk off together, sit down at a table, and get to work.

When I first started my fieldwork in Martha's classroom in early October, she and the children were in the early stages of a unit on the solar system. They had already done Mercury and Venus and were just beginning the moon. For each planet, the children were writing a report of facts with an illustration of the planet. The illustrations were all different, done with different media that reflect something about the nature of the surface of the planet. The moon's surface is sandy, so the children made their moons by brushing a circle of paper with glue and dipping it into sand. Then they made craters with more glue and sand. Mars is dry and dusty, so the children used chalk. The solar system unit activities occurred at several stations during each morning: the other stations had cooking projects, math activities, or art projects.

One day, some of the children were doing marble paintings at the art table. This is a common art activity in preschool and primary classrooms: children roll paint-covered marbles around on pieces of paper in the bottom of a shallow box, making random patterns of colored lines. Elsewhere in the room, other children were writing their Mars reports, making Mars landing modules, and working with unifix cubes. During meeting the next day, Martha started talking to the children about Jupiter—its size, its gaseous nature, and the way it looks, with striated bands of color. One of the activities for that morning was to trace a round circle on the back of yesterday's stripey marble painting and cut it out. And voilà! Jupiter! Often the full breadth and depth of Martha's activities revealed themselves to me slowly—today's marble painting becomes tomorrow's Jupiter, today's sculpted map of the surface of the moon becomes tomorrow's painting activity and Friday's landscape for home-made moon vehicles and elaborate space-landing adventures. Each step is a fully valuable activity unto itself, but the pieces fit together in a way that is artfully wrought and orchestrated.

Martha is passionate about her work. She plans carefully and attends to the minutest details. Not long before Halloween, she put out a math game for the children to play with during activity time. The game was simple, little more than a vehicle for getting the children to write basic mathematical word problems. But the game pieces that Martha designed made this activity incredibly inviting and engaging. The individual game boards were made of midnight blue construction paper with the silhouette of a black Victorian-style haunted house glued on. Martha had painted large flat beans orange on one side and white on the other. The orange sides were then painted with tiny jack-o'-lantern faces, the white sides with tiny ghost faces. Each child had just the right props for the telling of spooky Halloween math stories—three pumpkins went into the scary haunted house. Two ghosts came too. How many were in the house all together? The children moved their beans in and out of their haunted houses, flipped their beans over and started again. Several children spent the whole morning at that station, writing addition and subtraction problems. Martha's creativity made a mundane task very compelling.

No lesson is impossible for Martha: her ingenuity and resourcefulness enable her to realize almost any curricular idea she invents. The children made "astronaut space food" by mixing instant chocolate pudding mix and milk in a ziploc baggie: nip off the corner of the bag and suck out your meal just like Sally Ride did. During a lesson on Pluto, Martha told the children, "Pluto is so cold . . . and cold makes me think of . . . ." She paused. "Ice?" Rosie offered. "Not ice, but you're close. . . . Ice cream!" she said. The children gasped, then cheered, amazed at their good fortune: later that day they proceeded to make ice cream in individual containers made of empty juice cans and cut down milk cartons. During my time in Room 4 we made dreamcatchers, stargazers, even hilarious paper turkey helmets. Ignited during her years teaching at Kiddie City, the fire of Martha's imagination still burns bright.

But for all of her passion, attention, devotion, and thoughtfulness, Martha's presentation of these educational activities is surprisingly neutral. Martha values self-direction. The children in her class are required to take responsibility for themselves and make choices. As a result, she does not feel comfortable forcing an activity on the children. Like Moses's mother putting her beloved infant in a basket and floating him down the Nile with no idea of where he might end up, Martha works hard to select and invent the very best activities she can, and then describes them to the children simply and directly, leaving it up to them to decide whether or not they will engage. No hoopla, no expectations, no obligations.

Sometimes Martha's laissez-faire approach to the introduction of activities leads to their failure. If the children don't buy into a particular idea—making family banners, singing "Parents Are People," writing outer space dictionaries—the activity dies a lonely death, unmourned by the children or their teacher. As with discipline, classroom organization, and social concerns, the locus of responsibility lies with the children. Martha says:

> I don't feel so great as a teacher when I realize that I have a lot invested in a plan, and that's become more important to me than what [the children] choose to do with it. It's hard to let go of the plan, which I think is a good plan and I'm invested in because it is something that I chose to do, and I thought would be a good thing. And I thought would be interesting to them and appropriate. And yet when it doesn't come to fruition the way that I had expected, I like to be able to let go of what I expected, and to let them do with it whatever they need to do with it . . . . And also to not take that personally when it happens. And not to necessarily think that it is a bad plan, because I've tried those plans again with other classes and they've worked just fine, or I've done them with classes before. For whatever reason, the dynamics of the group, or whenever you choose to do it, or whatever I said when I presented it, or whatever the personalities are . . . I never have the upper hand. Always remember that!

Martha expends a lot of energy in the early stages of each lesson—planning, developing materials, arranging the environment—in order to build a firm foundation for the children's experience with the activity. Once the children begin to interact with the materials, the activity is out of her hands: its success or failure rests with the children. The intensity of Martha's passion for careful attention to detail is balanced by her commitment to letting go.

A side effect of this approach is that the children do not always have a strong sense of why they are doing the things they are doing. For example, one hectic morning right before Christmas vacation, in the midst of their unit on night, stars, and solstice, the children were given the opportunity to make cut-paper lanterns. Some of the children, like Robert and Dara, took this activity very seriously, and crafted their lanterns with care. Others, Carlos for example, did a perfunctory and sloppy job, eager to move on to free choice activities. And some, like Gus, simply did not make lanterns at all. Though these lanterns were certainly not the heart of the day's educational enterprise, they were linked to the unit's theme of night and darkness. The connection was there, but Martha made no mention of it.

Was the lantern project worth doing? Was it busywork? Why should the children bother with it? Martha made none of this clear. Even if lanterns were worth making, even if they made sense within the overall shape of the unit and enhanced the children's experience with the central concepts of the unit, Martha said nothing, leaving it up to the children to make their own connections.

❖❖❖❖❖❖

Martha states matter-of-factly that she learned to be a teacher by teaching at Kiddie City. Like many of us, Martha feels that her college training did little to prepare her for the real-world experience of her chosen profession. However, she admits that she did learn something. She said:

> I think that the one thing that I did gain —and I can remember my advisor saying this—was that you can teach anything to anybody. I can just remember, because I was trying to build something, some curriculum thing and I kept saying, "no, this is going to be too hard for them, this is going to be too hard." And he was just trying to tell me to just keep thinking about it and a way will come to you that will be appropriate.

Martha's advisor's advice, passed on to her in the early 1980s and clearly influenced by Jerome Bruner's assertion that "any subject can be taught effectively in some intellectually honest form to any child at any stage of development" (1960, 33), has been a driving force in her curriculum planning for her ungraded classroom.

In their classic book on nongraded elementary schools, Goodlad and Anderson state that "in the average first grade there is a spread of four years in pupil readiness to learn as suggested by mental age data" (1959, 3). In other words, "any realistic attempt to approximate the readiness of these individuals for school work must assume a four-year range in difficulty for what various children are able to do: work levels must be geared for two years below first-grade expectancies as well as for two years above" (1959, 6). If this is indeed the case for a straight first grade class, and given that the range of abilities housed at a particular grade level widens as the children get older (Goodlad and Anderson 1959), the implications for Martha's classroom situation are staggering. She is faced with the challenge of teaching an ability span of eight or nine years.

To meet this challenge, Martha plans activities, like the pattern block activity described earlier, that work on many different levels. In these cases all of the children do the same activity, but in different ways. Martha also develops a variety of materials on a given topic, thus allowing all of the children in the class to work within the curricular theme, but to do so at a level of sophistication and complexity appropriate for each one. As part of her planning, she identifies key concepts that she would like to convey to the children and proceeds from there, creating activities that will give her students access to and experience with those key concepts.

Martha also maintains a relaxed attitude toward the material she teaches. In our dialogue journal, Martha wrote:

> Content knowledge or fact knowledge is somewhat secondary to me than process knowledge and/or the experience of just having tried things out. I mean, what were facts or knowledge about the solar system may or may not be true in the next fifteen years (How crucially important is it that you can name the planets in order anyway? I'm not sure it ever did a lot for me, except that I found it was interesting and I found a lot out through the study).

Martha seems to conflate content and facts, and dismisses both as secondary to her main focus on process and experience. However, her classroom is replete with content, and it is her passion for meaningful content that makes her classroom environment so rich. Facts are less appealing to Martha, and it is facts that are relegated to second place behind process. Martha's commitment to process and experience is very much in keeping with NAEYC's standards of developmentally appropriate practice in early childhood educational environments: primary grade children, such as those in Martha's class, should be given opportunities to learn through interaction with materials that are "concrete, real, and relevant" (Bredekamp 1987, 69), and should be allowed to move at their own pace in acquiring skills and knowledge.

Martha's emphasis on process and experience has implications for evaluation for student learning. I asked Martha about this in our dialogue journal after a morning of team-teaching:

> When and how do you expect the kids to demonstrate their understanding of the key concepts in a unit? For example, we talked about genes today, and had the kids do their family eye color pages. But I don't know if they understood anything we said. I don't know if they

could apply the concepts . . . or which of them could and which couldn't. And then I started thinking about the solar system unit. The kids copied info into their planet books, but do you know how much the kids remember/understand/really know about each planet? Does this even matter to you?

My handwriting on these journal pages—enormous, sloppy, urgent—suggests that it matters deeply to me.

Martha replies:

> Aha! Now we come to the slippery, tricky stuff . . . . The simple two word answer to your questions is either "I don't" or "It depends." It depends on lots of things. First of all, it depends on *what* all my goals, reasons, etc. . . . for doing a given theme, activity, lesson are. Some have a specific skill, some are practicing processes (like reading, or writing), refining skills, some for content knowledge—most for some combination of things. Next it depends on *who*. I don't have the same expectations for all. I clearly don't expect Amy [a kinder with no previous school experience] to have the same understanding (or any for that matter) of genetics as Peter [a highly skilled second grader] but hopefully she'll at least consider her eye color and other family members' more carefully, and next time around on this topic for her something will connect. As for Peter, I don't expect he "understands" genetics, but now he's familiar with the word . . . . I guess that maybe makes me sound disorganized or not too vigilant about learning and assessment, but I feel quite strongly that I have a good sense of what they know, or maybe I don't care as much about it as I think I do.

Martha is strongly convinced that the value of meeting the needs of each child as a whole child far outweighs any obligation or responsibility to the content being taught.

Again, Martha's perspective is very much in keeping with the NAEYC standards of developmentally appropriate practice. Bredekamp (1987, 65) writes:

> Knowledge of age-appropriate expectations is one dimension of developmentally appropriate practice, but equally important is knowledge of what is individually appropriate for the specific children in a classroom. Although universal and predictable sequences of human development appear to exist, a major premise of developmentally appropriate practice is that each child is unique and has an individual pattern of timing and growth, as well as individual personality, learning style, and family background. . . . Enormous variance exists in the timing of individual development that is within the normal range.

Recognizing this enormous variance in her class, Martha feels comfortable letting go of rigid expectations for coverage of material. Instead, she attempts to cover the broad spectrum of her children's needs and abilities and focuses on growth rather than end-points. As she said:

> I have to take it sort of from where they come in at to what they're next able to do. Like, obviously, my goals in terms of Connor being able to interact appropriately with other children and enter social groups and aid somebody else are based on improving from wherever he started at. So my ultimate ending expectation for him might be different than for someone like Lauren, who had strong pro-social skills when she came in.

This attitude is also apparent in some of Martha's assessment procedures. For example, she asked the children to do some cutting with scissors at the start of the year: "I had all the kids cut along certain lines for me at the beginning of the year—a straight, a zigzag, a curve—to see where their cutting was at. I am looking for a big, long-term thing about how their cutting has changed over the course of the year in here." Children's progress will be evaluated in terms of the distance travelled from their personal starting point, rather than in terms of their ability to reach a predetermined, external standard.

Acknowledging and responding to individual differences is also a central part of Nel Noddings's feminist re/visioning of education. In *The Challenge to Care in Schools* (1992), Noddings suggests that no one should be required to take algebra, or a foreign language, or creative writing: each child's education should be tailored to his or her capabilities, interests, desires and goals. Nel Noddings and Martha George share an interest in operationalizing the ethic of care in their classrooms, and believe in putting students and their needs before all other concerns.

My concerns about assessment raised in our dialogue journal in my insistent, demanding scrawl relate to the twin issues of commitment to the children and commitment to the discipline. Is there some content that demands to be covered, that deserves to be covered? Does a teacher owe it to the children to expose them to particular issues or to the kinds of knowledge that will enrich and enhance their education? Martha's belief in the value of process and experience is a broad brush whose strokes obscure some of the subtleties of the situation.

On the very last day of my fieldwork in Martha's classroom, she and I sat down with a big blob of play-dough and started talking. We were sculpting representations of our teaching out of clay that Martha had made for the children to use during the unit on night, stars, and solstice. The clay was pitch black and full of glitter: starry night play-dough. This sculpting activity was done during Christmas vacation in Martha's empty classroom. The classroom felt eery: no children, no noise, no heat, no life. Almost a ghost town. We sat on the rug in the meeting area, kneading and shaping. I had specifically asked Martha if we could do this activity with this particular batch of clay because it is fraught with insight into Martha's teaching.

I had never seen black clay before. I had never even imagined black clay. This black clay had sprung from the deep well of Martha's passion and creativity, just like the astronaut space food.

It is not easy to make black clay, since the food coloring teachers use to tint homemade play-dough won't blend into black. It gets pretty dark, but not really black. And not-really-black is not black enough for Martha. She is a perfectionist about things relating to her work, attending to every detail, and it mattered to her that the night play-dough be truly black. In our dialogue journal she wrote: "If I hold the value that I want the children to give me their best— I should give them mine."

So Martha made the huge batch of clay on her stove at home, using the same pots she cooks in. She used tempera paint to blacken the clay: her husband came home to find a sinkful of inky black pots, pans, spoons, and measuring cups. But he didn't blink an eye: this was not the first time that the boundaries between school and home had been blurred. Martha's classroom is full of small appliances borrowed from her kitchen cupboards— popcorn poppers, electric skillets—and her home bookcases have been denuded to fill the shelves of her classroom. Martha's commitment to teaching colors her life the way her black clay colored her cookware.

When we finished our sculptures, I packed up my things and got ready to leave. Martha straightened up her room, putting books onto shelves and reorganizing piles of student work. She came over to me with a baggie full of starry night play-dough. "Take this home for Sam," she said, referring to my two-year-old son. "Are you sure? What about your students? It's their clay," I replied. "Nah! That's okay. Go ahead. I think Sam will really love it," Martha answered, thinking, as usual, about the needs, interests, and desires of someone else's young child.

# 3
# Teacherly Love and Motherly Love

When I conceived this study, my original plan was to begin by spending a period of time as a participant observer in Martha's classroom, continue by joining her as a full-fledged partner in teaching, and then revert to being a participant observer again and phase myself slowly out of the life of her classroom. The first and last sections of the study would allow me to observe and study Martha's teaching, and to explore the contribution that love made to her teaching practices. The middle section of the study was designed to enable me to engage in similar observation and reflection on my own teaching practices. I expected that this design would give me two views of love's contribution to teaching. Martha and I were different types of people, and though we shared a philosophical orientation and a commitment to letting our love for children play a role in all facets of our teaching lives, I knew that this shared foundation would manifest itself differently in the lived reality of our individual teaching styles.

Observing Martha and participating in the life of the classroom was fascinating and fruitful. And I was so eager to teach children again. But when it came time for me to be Martha's co-teacher, things just didn't go as I had expected. I made a startling discovery: I could not really co-teach with Martha. I could develop curriculum. I could plan lessons. I could make up class poetry charts, create story frames, type up final copies of students' writing. I could mix paint. I could develop homework assignments. I could lead meeting. I could work with students on mathematics, writing, art, social studies, anything. I could teach the whole class. I could teach a small group. I could work one-on-one with a child. I could read stories and sing with the class. I could assess student work. And I did all of those things, and more besides. I felt very much at home in the classroom, very much a part of the class. The students even came to think of me as one of their teachers: in the achingly beautiful farewell book created for me when my fieldwork ended, Roseanne, one of the children, wrote "You are one of my favret teachers."

But I still did not feel like a teacher. Prior to my time in Martha's classroom I would have thought that doing all of those things were the heart of my profession. But I was doing all of those things, and yet I still didn't feel like a teacher. This was a big surprise, a frightening surprise, one that rattled the very core of my research design. So I rushed to the literature on qualitative research methods hoping to find a solution to what felt like a terrible problem.

I didn't find a solution, but I found a seemingly self-contradictory notion appearing again and again: During fieldwork, expect the unexpected (Glesne and Peshkin 1992; Eisner 1991; Wolcott 1990b, among others). Elliot Eisner, an expert on qualitative inquiry, writes: "Flexibility, adjustment, and iterativity are three hallmarks of qualitative 'method.' Even aims may change in the course of inquiry, depending upon what happens in the situation. Such an attitude toward method is diametrically opposed to the aspiration to bring everything under control so that effects can be unambiguously explained" (1991, 170).

No matter how carefully you plan, then, your reality is bound to be different from theory. Sometimes the difference between your plan and your experience is a simple shift in focus. While gathering her dissertation data, Jenifer Helms (1995) found that the questions she planned to examine regarding the current debates in science studies (such as realism versus antirealism, the nature of objectivity and scientific progress) were much less interesting to her and to the teachers she worked with than exploring the areas of intersection between science as a discipline, the teachers as individual people, and the act of teaching science. As a result, the dissertation that she wrote is different from the one she had planned to write.

Sometimes the unexpected looms much, much larger. Perhaps the most enormous example of this is Harry Wolcott's case study of an underachieving, disenfranchised young adult whom he referred to as a "sneaky kid" (1990). Unexpectedly, Wolcott's research relationship with this sneaky kid turned into a sexual relationship. Then the unexpected returned in a plot twist almost too bizarre to comprehend. The sneaky kid, attempting to murder Wolcott, burns his house to the ground.

My methodological problem seemed small and manageable, almost friendly, in the shadow of Wolcott's story. I felt that I must be on the right track, methodologically speaking, if my time in Martha's classroom was causing me to rethink my preconceived plans. Again, Eisner writes: ". . . [I]n qualitative studies, researchers take their cues from what emerges; it is not unusual for qualitative researchers to have only a general, even a vague, idea about the directions or course of action they will take until they experience the setting. . . . In a school the qualities 'unfurl' and the qualitative researcher sees and selects" (1991, 172).

As things unfurled in Martha's classroom, I realized that in order to examine fully the contributions made by love to my own teaching, I would have to do two things. I would reflect on my experience in Martha's classroom and analyze the aspects of my practice that were enacted there, as I had originally planned. But I would also need to go back and explore the contributions that love made to my teaching when I myself was the teacher of record. During my final year as a second grade teacher in Loma Prieta, I kept a reflective journal. Each day after recess the children and I would sit down at our desks for 15 minutes and write. I always wrote in my journal when I asked the children to write in theirs: it was important to me as a teacher to let them see an adult writing, and to demonstrate to them that I really believed journal writing to be a worthwhile endeavor. So my purpose in keeping this reflective journal was not to collect data for a future study—I was accepted into a graduate program in education in March of that year, and had been journaling for many months and, as a result, the daily entries are as likely to be about yesterday's crummy staff meeting, my new bicycle, the children's behavior, or the upcoming Grateful Dead concerts as about deeper issues in education. However, the entries which focus on curriculum, on philosophy, and on love and my students are very revealing, with a level of immediacy that comes from deep and unselfconscious immersion in practice.

Using these journals raises some important issues. There are significant differences between my experience as a classroom teacher and my experiences as a teacher in someone else's classroom. Loving teaching is very specific, coupled tightly with the particular children and the particular setting. The feelings I had for the children discussed in my journal are bound to be different from the feelings I had for the children in Martha's class:

different children will naturally evoke different feelings. Second, when I was the teacher of record I had very different reasons to love my students than I had when I entered Martha's classroom. Third, I had more time each day and over the course of the school year to allow my feelings to grow and deepen. Now, I do suspect that there are certain features of teaching with love that are specific to me, and which would manifest themselves in any teaching setting. But I also believe that there are important aspects of my loving teaching practices that could not be given an opportunity to surface within the constraints of this research experience: I used my own teaching journals, then, as a source of data on aspects of love in my teaching that I was unable to access in Martha's classroom.

From my very first weeks in the teaching profession, I found it impossible to avoid falling in love with my students. My professional conscience led me to focus on the children as emotional, feeling beings, and required my presence as an emotional, feeling being as well. My commitment to their development and growth demanded that I enter into a relationship with each of them. Chris Zajac, the fifth grade teacher in Tracy Kidder's *Among Schoolchildren*, deliberately chose never to use the word love to describe her relationship with her students, believing that "it would be very dangerous to feel toward strangers' children who were merely passing through her life that particular attachment and all the hopes that 'love' implied" (Kidder 1989, 159). Protection was her motivation: "If she let a student into that special circle of her affections, she would resent him if he called her a bitch"(Kidder 1989, 159). While I am very uncomfortable with Zajac's twist on the situation, my teaching journal entries for the last few weeks of school are rife with indications that my love for my students was leading to sadness and pain at the year's end:

Teaching Journal 5/22/91
I love my students up, down, and sideways and I dread the end of the year. . . .


Teaching Journal 6/6/91
If I had only liked Alesha instead of allowing myself to love her, I would not feel so sad. It would have helped with Roberto too, last year.

Teaching Journal 6/22/91
The last journals of second grade. Hard to believe! I can't take all this
looking back, singing "Circle Game," etc. Too emotionally exhausting.

Though loving students was inevitably a bittersweet
experience, it never felt like a choice: I felt that it was my
responsibility as a teacher to love each child. This commitment
was a crucial part of my professional conscience. Love did not
happen spontaneously in many cases, and sometimes required a
focused effort, as this journal excerpt illustrates:

Teaching Journal 10/18/90
Elliot is very . . . . I don't know. Test-y. Likes to push. Maybe he thinks
because he's smart he can bend the rules, talk without cease, be sassy, etc.
I've never used the phrase "too big for his britches," but it fits here. How
can I not get frustrated and start to dislike him? I want to like him—I
want to love him, and I know that I can. But he's not making himself
lovable to me. Not right now.

But when I got to Martha's classroom, I found it almost
impossible to love the children. I tried. I reminded myself that
teaching is like an arranged marriage: what is important at the
outset is not so much love as the commitment to love. I reminded
myself of Elliot and some of the other children in my past who
had taken some time to love. I tried to delight in the children's
wonderful personalities. I tried to love their laughter, their energy,
their poetry, their artwork. Nothing happened. I was supposed
to be doing my research on the role of love in my teaching and if I
couldn't come to love these children I would have nothing to write
about: I developed loving-teacher performance anxiety. I started
to worry. Maybe graduate school had stolen my soul, turning me
into a heartless academic and destroying the teacher in me.
Maybe it was my own children's fault. When I had taught second
grade prior to graduate school, I was childless. Did I only love
my students then because I had no children of my own? Maybe it
wasn't possible to be a mother and a loving teacher at the same
time. Maybe that was too much to ask. So I decided to forget
about love and think about teaching instead. I hoped that the
experience of teaching children would lead to the development of
loving feelings.

In their handbook on the process and experience of becoming a
qualitative researcher, Glesne and Peshkin suggest that you must

tap into your subjectivity and passion to find a research question that will be intriguing and motivating. Though they warn novice researchers about the occasionally blurry line between "a topic for research and a topic for psychoanalysis," the authors suggest that, as a researcher, you should examine the ways that "your proposed research arises out of your life history" (Glesne and Peshkin 1992, 14).

My interest in the role of love in the education of young children is certainly linked closely to my professional life history. From the start of my teaching career, I considered loving children to be the backbone of my practice. I earned my teaching credential in a program that was primarily designed for in-service teachers studying to obtain a master's degree, and, as a result, skipped over all of the basics of teacher education. I had read only one one book on the subject of general curriculum, Herb Kohl's *The Open Classroom* (1969), prior to beginning my doctoral work. It was loaned to me by my student teaching supervisor, and it fit me like a glove.

"Our schools are crazy," Kohl writes. He continues:

> They do not serve the interests of adults, and they do not serve the interests of young people. They teach "objective" knowledge and its corollary, obedience to authority. They teach avoidance of conflict and obeisance to tradition in the guise of history. They teach equality and democracy while castrating students and controlling teachers. Most of all they teach people to be silent about what they think and feel, and worst of all, they teach people to pretend that they are saying what they think and feel. To try to break away from stupid schooling is no easy matter for teacher or student. (1969, 116)

Beneath this occasionally inflammatory and clearly dated rhetoric was sound guidance for creating a nonauthoritarian learning environment rooted in respect for children and for the wisdom they possess. Kohl taught me that "it is essential to listen to the voice of the students"(Kohl 1969, 27). He taught me that "there is no one way to learn" (Kohl 1969, 52), and that I should celebrate "creative disorder" (Kohl 1969, 39). He assured me to be myself in the classroom, and to trust myself and my students. He made it clear that there was room for passion in teaching.

Nowhere does Kohl state that teachers should love their students. But Kohl's writings encouraged me to have confidence in my instincts. I wanted to love my students, and Kohl gave me permission. So I left my atypical teacher training experience in 1989, firmly believing that love for children was an appropriate basis for curricular decision making. No one had told me otherwise. I did not know the degree to which Kohl had veered from the path carved by more conventional writers on education.

Herb Kohl was not the only influence on the development of my teaching philosophy to be found slightly off the beaten path of educational research. During my first years as a teacher, my husband was studying for a graduate degree in business. Though I am always quick to resist any associations between the world of teaching and the world of business, I found that some of the ideas that my husband brought home made a great deal of sense in the life of my classroom.

Most influential was the work of Jim Collins.[7] A world-class rock climber and well-regarded management consultant, Collins taught a wildly popular business school class in small business management that emphasized the importance of mission statements for businesses. Collins believed that a mission statement should be more than a string of platitudes about quality, excellence, and customer satisfaction—it should be a strong, clearly articulated and well-defined statement that captures the vision of the company. The mission statement should be a powerful tool, used as a daily part of conducting business.

I was intrigued by this idea. My school had an official mission statement, but it was little more than a page on our California State School Report Card, and it was indistinguishable from the mission statements of most of the other schools in our district. It had no impact on our teaching or on the daily lives of our classrooms: once we had spent fifteen minutes of a faculty meeting writing it, we never looked at it again. It seemed very worthwhile to have a clearly articulated statement of my beliefs about education and teaching, and so I attempted to develop one for myself, writing the following in my journal:

Teaching Journal 11/28/90
. . . . and child-centered is me. The affective needs of the kids are the heart. Of course, the content is important, as are the skills the child develops, but inherent in and basic to everything that goes on is an awareness of

---

[7]Further explication of the ideas described here, along with much of the content of Jim Collins's course, can be found in Collins and Lazier (1994).

the kids as people. Validating their opinions, encouraging them to think, to wonder, to question, to ask, to agree or disagree; affirming their senses of self, and developing their personal and intellectual self-confidence; nurturing their curiosity and their love of life and learning; demanding and modelling responsible, kind behavior; fostering interdependence as well as independence—these are what I'm all about. All these things underlie the teaching of skills and the communication of academic content.

Collins believed that a good mission statement could guide policy and decision making. In a company with a powerful mission statement, any worker anywhere in the organization could make any kind of business decision simply by evaluating the situation in light of the company's mission. For example, if the company's mission was to provide customers with prompt service and good value, an employee could ask herself "would this solution enhance our ability to provide our customers with prompt service and good value?" If the answer was no, then the decision was already made.

I felt that this made perfect sense for teaching. Be clear about your passions and about what you value. Articulate your mission, your vision, your foundation, and then make your professional decisions accordingly. I elaborated upon this in my journal:

> Teaching Journal 4/29/91
> For example, my foundation involves affirming each student's importance and capabilities, and centers on issues relating to social responsibility, empowerment, respect for self and others, and critical thought. Consequently I try to make sure that every single activity that I do with my students reflects these principles. *That's* why I hate the CTBS [the California Test of Basic Skills, a standardized achievement test]. It doesn't take the children's needs into account, *and* it doesn't reflect my strongly held beliefs.
>
> I feel accountable to myself and to my vision of what a classroom should be. . . . How can I teach reading in a manner consistent with my beliefs? How can I manage my classroom in a manner consistent with my beliefs? Any educational decision I make, I evaluate against that yardstick. No other yardstick had meaning for me. . . EVERYTHING should be consistent and aligned, and everything will reinforce everything else! . . . I feel very responsible, and very capable of making any decision based on my professional conscience.

I hated the California Test of Basic Skills because, like all standardized, fill-in-the-bubble tests, it left no room for creativity, for subtle nuance, for critical reinterpretation. It did not test what I taught, nor what I valued, nor what I knew to be important for children and their intellectual development. And I hated the idea that the bright, wonderful, special children in my class were almost guaranteed poor scores: in their time in my classroom they had almost never been asked to come up with the one right answer for a question, and they only rarely had to fill in a blank on a worksheet. If they did poorly on the CTBS, then, it would be my fault for not preparing them. But I could not, and would not, prepare them to engage in a type of activity that I felt was developmentally inappropriate, demoralizing, and generally unnecessary.

The philosophy that I articulated in my teaching journal entry of 11/28/90 had taken on a life of its own. It stopped being a simple mission statement and became a passion, "my professional conscience." I had taken my love for children and my belief that love could constitute a legitimate foundation for the education of young children and put them to the test in the classroom. As I taught, my experiences helped to clarify and solidify my beliefs. Through the experience of teaching, my notions were transformed into knowledge.

In the same way that feminist philosophers have rooted the ethic of care in the experience of mothering, my ideas about love and teaching children spring from my experience as a teacher. And Martha, too, arrived at her commitment to teach with love as a fundamental guiding force through her own lived experience as a classroom teacher. This confidence in the value of the practical as a source of knowledge is closely linked to the community of feminist thought. Dorothy Smith (1987), for example, calls for a sociology that would be rooted firmly in the everyday world, exploring the problematic nature of our ordinary lives. This position is also gaining in popularity in the educational research community (Richardson 1994).

Jean Clandinin, for example, is the foremost advocate of respect for the knowledge that grows out of teaching practices. She refers to this type of knowledge as "personal practical knowledge," a type of knowledge that is "experiential, value-laden, purposeful, and oriented to practice" (Clandinin 1986, 20). Clandinin asserts that teachers learn by teaching, accruing not only experience but also knowledge. She exhorts the educational research community to acknowledge personal practical knowledge as a valid source of information about teachers and teaching. My knowledge about love and its contribution to education is an example of Clandinin's concept of personal practical knowledge.

One of the purposes of this study was to explore one aspect of my personal practical knowledge—namely the use of love as a foundation for teaching—and the personal practical knowledge of another teacher with a similar philosophy, and to look for themes, patterns, gaps, and differences in experience and interpretation. Thinking back to Glesne and Peshkin's warning about careful selection of questions for inquiry, then, it seems that I had selected a research topic that was close to my heart, to be sure, but also close to my mind and to the minds of other scholars.

❖ ❖ ❖ ❖ ❖ ❖

In my first week in Martha's classroom, I decided to spend one day looking not at what was there, but at what was missing. In doing so I learned nothing about Martha's teaching practices but a great deal about my own:

> Today I am going to spend some time writing about what I feel is missing here (or what I haven't found yet)
> 1) no whole group experiences . . .
> 2) no time when all the kids are focused on one child's words or work . . .
> 3) singing . . .
> 4) content. I know that lots goes on here when I'm not here, but I still think there could be more.
> 5) hugging. Martha is not an effusive person by any means, but I expected to see more overt expressions of intimacy, of caring.
> (Field Notes 10/13/94)

Clearly, I had come to Martha's classroom with a preconceived idea of what loving education would look like, an idea that was rooted in my own experience as a classroom teacher. I felt almost disappointed when I watched her teach and felt that things were missing: I had storied her (Clandinin, Davies, Hogan, and Kennard 1993) to be "perfect" or, in other, more incriminating, words, just like me. Of course, what I felt was missing from Martha's classroom experience was not really missing. Martha's teaching practices were simply different from mine, and certain things that mattered deeply to me were not all that important to her.   When I was jarred by practices and experiences that were different from what I had expected, I became acutely aware of my preconceptions and biases.  I learned that loving education is not a monolithic entity: it was unrealistic to think that there would be one right way to incorporate love into the teaching of young children.

In our final debriefing at the end of our time together, Martha touched on this same issue.  She said:

> Despite the fact that I had no reservations about having you come and all of that, when you first started coming, I was very nervous.  Way nervous.  Like, Oh God, she thinks all these great things, what if she sees just s-h-i-t when she comes in here.  Or what if I'm not what she expected?  What if I talk a good talk and don't walk the walk or whatever.

I thought this was just Martha's typical self-deprecating humor, but worried that there was some truth beneath it.  So I asked her if she really thought that this had been a possibility. "Yeah," she replied:

> Not a possibility that you would have thought that I was a horrible teacher, because I think that in all of the discussions that we have had, philosophically we're in the same place.  But there was the real kind of worry that it would be manifested so differently in something that I would do than in something that you would do, and . . . sometimes people don't make that jump.

Though I was able to make that jump, it took me a while.  And I was always intrigued by our differences in understanding, interpreting and responding to situations.  For example, early in my time in Martha's classroom, I observed an interaction within a group of students working on individual projects at the same learning station.  Mark was creating an illustration for his story, copying a drawing from a book.  Peter came over and said that he was using the book; a disagreement ensued.  Roseanne sided with Peter, Mark became defensive.  The children's words became harsher and nastier.  My inclination was to step in and stop the argument with a blanket proclamation along the lines of "we do not speak to each other that way in this classroom" and to offer them guidance in finding some acceptable solution to their problem.  But Martha did nothing.  She stood by silently and watched as tensions mounted.  It was all I could do to hold myself back, but Martha busied herself with other things, allowing them time to work out the problem on their own. When it seemed that Mark was about to cry, Roseanne and Peter relented, and asked Martha for some help in negotiating a compromise.

My instincts told me to intervene, Martha's told her to hold off. My code of classroom etiquette calls for protecting the feelings of all the members of the community. The rights of each individual (e.g., Peter's right to use the drawing book) are overshadowed by responsibility to the community. Martha's code calls for encouraging children to take responsibility for their own actions and to solve their own problems, turning to other children for help and support before asking an adult. Both of our responses would have been appropriate and acceptable, and both are rooted in our love for children and our vision of what a loving classroom should be like. We shared an intent—to respond to these types of situations in a loving manner—but our interpretations of this intent, our reactions, differed.

Because I was a guest in Martha's classroom, I learned to respond and to react in a way that would be compatible and consistent with the value system of her classroom: it was important to me that the children receive clear messages about acceptable behavior. At first it was difficult to put aside my gut-level, genuine, teacherly response to a situation and react differently. But doing so helped me to see important differences between Martha's vision of a loving classroom and my own.

But is it enough to share an intent? What if Martha's response had been to threaten the children, or to hit them, or to humiliate them before the class? If those responses had been rooted in a love of children and a desire to do the right thing for them, would that make them all right? One of the hidden dangers in the word "love" is that it means many different things to different people. Martha and I spoke about this ambiguity problem. She said:

> I've heard a million teachers say "Oh, I'm a teacher because I love children." You love what? You love manipulating them? You love making them cut out all the same things? You love having power over them? So, I think it's really hard, just (pause) I don't think that asking a teacher, "Do you love your children?" would be enough. I think that you would really have to know what their definition of loving children or loving teaching or whatever was.

It is important, then, in loving education to be clear and explicit about your beliefs and values. It is crucial to avoid what

Alice Miller (1983, 3) calls "poisonous pedagogy," the syndrome of doing harm to children, physically or psychologically, and then thinking you have done so "for their own good." The notion of teaching with love is complicated by these issues. It is clear that there are certain behaviors and ways of thinking that are acceptable and others that are obviously pathological. But the borderlands, the precise boundaries between right and wrong, appropriate and inappropriate, child-serving and adult-serving, are cloudy, shrouded in a silent haze of ambiguity.

On the day that I was looking for what was "missing" in Martha's classroom, I wrote the following in my journal:

> The children rarely all do the same thing at the same time. Is there a loss of group identity as a result? Is there a sense of "us" here? . . . Or do I just feel that there's not much of a sense of community because I am on the outside? . . . And where is the singing? I can see evidence of shared poems, but what about songs? I think singing is such an important part of the ECE experience. Also, I always used songs to build community and shared experience (among other things). . . .
> (Field Notes 10/13/94)

My observations about the lack of whole group experiences in Martha's classroom and my concern about the development of "a sense of us" point directly to a central issue in my own teaching. Inspired, perhaps, by Herb Kohl, who wrote, "[M]y students and I resembled a community much more than a class, and I enjoyed being with them" (1969, 14), I considered the development of community, of a shared ethos in the classroom, to be the heart of my professional life. In my teaching journal I returned again and again to the subject of developing community:

> Teaching Journal 9/12/90
> I want to love these kids. I really do. I know that it takes time, but I wish that the getting-to-know-you time had passed already.

I felt uncomfortable at the start of the year, as uncomfortable as a brand new pair of back-to-school shoes. I had my passion for teaching and my commitment to love, but I needed more. I was yearning for the connection, the intimacy, that would make my loving feelings balanced and complete. However, after just a few days, I wrote:

Teaching Journal 9/24/90
So last Thursday it started to happen, and on Friday it was official. This class jelled—I love them. As a whole: I still need to work and learn to love them as individuals. They're feeling more like a group now—it shows in the way they relate to one another. All the experiences we share—songs, jokes, events, laughter, music & movements [music and movement is the name of a dance curriculum that I developed and used with my students]—they build and build into something really neat and beautiful. It's that rhythm, that harmony, that *consonance* that make life in Room 6 so wonderful. And it was the absence of that quality which made (makes? is making?) the beginning of the year so hard. I need to make an effort to build community, shared decision making, responsibility toward oneself and one's "group" (if that is what we are to be called)—a sense of us-ness. Build an *us* that is to be treasured—a whole way greater than the sum of its parts.

Reading these entries now, it seems that establishing relationship with the students and among the students was my primary goal at the start of the school year: it was as if I did not feel like a teacher until that had happened. Though I referred to it as building community, this phenomenon can also be looked at as the development of intimacy, a critical component of teaching with love.

Developing and nurturing this community of learners was also one of my greatest sources of professional satisfaction. After I decided to leave teaching to go to graduate school, I reflected on my teaching experience in my journal:

Teaching Journal 4/29/91
My recent revelations have been many. They were all started by my terrible, gut-wrenching ambivalence about leaving the classroom. I thought a lot about what I value and what specifically I'll miss. Last year I believed that I had the best class in the school, and that's what made the year so extraordinary. My focus was on the specific children. I thought (even at the beginning of this year) that I'd never again have the magical experience I had with my first class—the shared sense of us-ness, the special love we had for each other, the willingness to be responsible for one another. But now I see that it is *not* really a function of the individual children and their personalities and gifts. Although I do love the individual children and cherish their personalities and gifts, what I really get off on, what really sends me, is the process of taking a bunch of individuals and turning them (us) into a cohesive group, a community with a culture all its own. Building a family of learners (and working to include parents and sibs) with its own history, set of rules, lingo, songs, rituals, etc. I create my own world, a world in which children are respected, cared for, encouraged, challenged and AFFIRMED AND VALIDATED. Could I do this with any group of children? Maybe.

> Probably. But it's the process of creating our class that I love and will miss so much—the process of creating a tribe: tribogenesis.

Orchestrating this process of "tribogenesis" was central to my image of myself as a teacher. One manifestation of the commitment to allow love to play a role in my teaching is my use of the phrase "a family of learners." It was not enough for us to be a community. Our connections ran deeper, and were more emotional, more intimate—we were a family.

One of the reasons I was unable to truly feel like a teacher in Martha's classroom was because I could not direct that process of "tribogenesis." Of course, a sense of community did develop during the months that I spent in Martha's classroom, with no help/interference from me. Even Martha felt that she played only a very minor role in its development: "I think you can lay all the groundwork . . . , but I don't think it's really overt things that you do that make it happen. . . . [It] happens quite naturally." In Martha's classroom, a sense of community arises gradually from the children and their own initiative and experience, rather than from the teacher's efforts.

Typically, Martha felt that her contribution to the development of community was to get out of the way and allow it to happen. Because I felt so strongly about taking an active role in the development of the culture of my classroom, I found that hard to accept. In our conversations and in our dialogue journal I kept asking Martha questions about the steps she took to build community. I asked the same question in many different forms, and was often surprised by the answers I received.

Martha spoke about doing conflict resolution with the olders as a way to build community: "I've started more stuff in the afternoons because the olders were more ready to sit and talk about those things, and have longer meetings and stuff than the youngers were ready to." Shocked, I asked, "So you're doing things that build a sense of community without having the whole community present?"

We discussed this situation again in a later conversation. Martha's elaboration illustrates the fact that while she values community, her primary commitment is to the needs of the children as individuals:

> It's hard, but at the same time I know that, while I would carry Robert and some of the [kinders], Maria and Gus would just make that

impossible. . . . I mean they wouldn't be there anyway, and that makes me
feel bad when I try to start something like that that is just too (pause)—
it's not at an appropriate level for them. Because then my expectations
that I would impose on them for sitting and listening are not realistic.
That's not appropriate for me to be doing either. . . . Obviously,
developmentally it's not appropriate for them.

Though community is important to Martha, the children and
their abilities and capabilities take precedence.

Unlike Martha, I did not step back and allow community to
develop on its own.  In my own classroom, I often worked hard to
develop a sense of shared values and experiences to bond the
class together and to bond them to me.  I felt responsible for the
creation of my tribe, as my 4/29/92 teaching journal entry
indicates—"I create my own world . . ."—and was willing to take
center stage and be directive in order to do so.   This is another
example of  Martha and me sharing a goal—in this case the
creation of a caring community in the classroom—just using
different routes to get there.

But is it also an example of poisonous pedagogy?  I was trying
to create a certain feeling or ethos in my classroom, mainly
because I believed that it would be conducive to a positive
environment for learning.  It was "for their own good," in other
words.  Alice Miller's book on the hidden cruelty in child-rearing,
*For Your Own Good* (1983), suggests that it is necessary to take a
closer look at this issue.  She writes about manipulation, and the
ways that pedagogy can be used to meet the needs of adults
rather than children.  Miller paints a chilling portrait of a
controlling teacher by quoting Jean-Jacques Rousseau (*Emile*, Book
II):

> Take an opposite route with your pupil; always let him think he is the
> master, but always be it yourself.  There is no more perfect form of
> subjection than the one that preserves the appearance of freedom; thus
> does the will itself become captive.  The poor child, who knows nothing,
> who can do nothing, and has no experience—is he not at your mercy?
> Are you not in control of everything in his environment that relates to
> him?  Can you not control his impressions as you please?  His tasks, his
> games, his pleasures, his troubles—is all this not in your hands without
> his knowing it?  Doubtlessly, he may do as he wishes, but he may wish
> only what you want him to; he may not take a single step that you have
> not anticipated, he may not open his mouth without your knowing what
> he is going to say. (quoted in Miller 1983, 97)

Miller's work raises questions about my teaching practices. Was I using my students? Was I abusing my power as their teacher? Was I using my classroom as a forum for the working through of my own psychological issues? Was I little more than a wolf in sheep's clothing, manipulating the children in the name of community? Perhaps, but I certainly hope not. At least, that was not my intent. I feel confident that my desired outcome, a sense of community in the classroom, was worthwhile. And the route I chose to get there, the deliberate and calculated fostering of shared experience, fell well within the range of to-be-expected responsibilities of a teacher. I thought that no one was harmed by my efforts to build community, although Alice Miller's psychoanalytic perspective might suggest otherwise. Miller's work serves as a reminder: loving teachers must make their decisions carefully and consciously, always engaging in vigilant reflection.

❖ ❖ ❖ ❖ ❖ ❖

During my first month in Martha's classroom, I thought a great deal about my feelings for the children. The journal I kept is full of doubt:

> I find it hard to imagine loving these kids. Will I be able to be a loving teacher? . . . I thought that being a mom would make it easier, somehow, to love other people's children. But right now at least, I feel very closed down to these kids.
> (Field Notes 10/11/94)

It seemed like love would never happen. But I was optimistic:

> I don't feel love for them right now, but I am committed to acting as if I love them. I expect that this will lead to the development of real loving feelings.
> (Field Notes 10/24/94)

I would rely on commitment and passion for the time being, while hoping and waiting for intimacy. I tried not to worry about love and to focus instead on Martha's teaching practices, helping out in the classroom in any way possible. I expected that things would improve when we moved into the co-teaching portion of the study and I was more directly involved with the children. Relationships would develop, I hoped. Then, on Halloween I realized that I already had relationships with Martha's students, and that my feelings for them were much stronger than I had realized.

Halloween is surely one of the worst days to be a teacher. The children are frantic with candy lust, their hearts and minds far away from the classroom. Chaos reigns supreme, and even the most routine and mundane tasks become a struggle to complete. But the children love it so. Martha and I decided that we were determined to enjoy our classroom Halloween celebrations as much as possible. We dressed up as identical twins, much to the children's delight. Martha planned an engaging array of activities for the children to do after the morning's all-school Halloween Costume Parade: scooping and carving class pumpkins, using candy corn to do a mathematics activity relating to area and perimeter of drawn jack-o'-lanterns, decorating cookies, and cutting out and assembling jointed skeletons.

The Halloween Costume Parade was a nightmare. The whole school gathered on the playground to share their costumes. Alexander, the principal, was armed with a classic piece of elementary school administrational equipment: a malfunctioning megaphone. His instructions were indecipherable, lost in a cloud of feedback, echo, and volume distortions. And then suddenly it was time for the parade, which has traditionally gone off the school grounds and around the corner. Like water breaking through a dam and flooding a residential neighborhood, the children burst out of the schoolyard and into the street. The children from Room 4 had not been assembled together when the parade began, and as the stream of children—all rather unrecognizable in their costumes—rushed and swirled around me, I tried frantically to find our kids, eager to keep them together and to keep them safe.

Was that masked child one of ours? What about that red Power Ranger? Isn't that Mitchell? No, too tall. Maybe that red Power Ranger is Mitchell. Or that one. I whirled around, counting heads. What was Lauren wearing? Oh, okay, I see her, and I see Li Ping. She's holding Chihoe's hand, and there's Kristen. Good. And I see that six or seven of them are up ahead with Martha.

The younger children were just swept along in the current. Amy, a kindergartner dressed as a fairy princess, grabbed onto the edge of my T-shirt and looked up at me with eyes big as saucers. "Where are we GOING?!?!" she cried. I took her hand as the parade continued, as much for my own benefit as for hers. Though the costumes and the pace of the parade had blurred the children's identities, I scanned the crowd as Amy and I walked along, making a somewhat futile attempt to locate more of our kids.

We rounded the corner, went into the parking lot of a neighborhood church, and found our way through a break in the fence back into Bayview's playground. My heart was pounding as we returned to Room 4. Though I had no official responsibility for the safety and well-being of this group of children, I cared about them, each of them. My feelings of connection to them were as compelling as any official responsibility could be. The children reappeared slowly but surely, took off their costumes, and got to work at the activities Martha had set out for them. I counted heads one last time, relieved that our children were all back where they belonged. I looked around the room and saw Brian, still in his ninja suit, clutching a fistful of candy corn and bent over a drawing of a jack-o'-lantern. He was hard at work, his tongue sticking out of his mouth in concentration, covering his picture with candies, hoping that his estimate was correct. I sat down beside him and got to work, offering encouragement, answering questions, teaching.

Commitment to love Martha's children did lead to the development of genuine feelings, as I had hoped and expected. As Sternberg's (1988a) work on love suggests, commitment is an important component of love.

Some of the children were so eager to enter into a friendship with me: Chihoe rushed to sit next to me during morning meetings, Rosie cuddled up against me, thumb in mouth, any chance she got, Connor held my hand as we walked to the book fair. Mitchell told me all about his Captain Picard action figure, and Mark told me about his blue bathrobe, the one he wears after he goes swimming. Amy asked me to read with her. Dara asked me about my children, and Li Ping read me the story she had written.

With memories of Alice Miller and poisonous pedagogy fresh in my mind, I worried that it was manipulative of me to try to love them, to ask them to establish relationships with me, simply for the sake of my research agenda. In my career as a classroom teacher, the children and I had good reasons to love, to invest in each other emotionally. But what about Martha's students? I'm not their real teacher—what reason could they possibly have to invest their emotions in me? After I nervously asked Martha about this in our dialogue journal, she responded: "Does it have to do with youth and innocence? Perhaps children only need reasons NOT to love or care for people, and are otherwise willing to open themselves and their hearts."

Martha's words made sense. After a few days of reflection, I again wrote in my journal, trying to resolve this problematic issue:

> [In the context of this study] it is not evil for me to offer love to these kids, and if relationships develop that is only an enrichment of their learning lives. I don't need to feel bad about that.
> (Field Notes 10/25/94)

Though I still didn't quite feel that I loved the students in Martha's class, I did have warm, positive feelings about most of them. Some of them, however, expressed no interest in developing a relationship with me. Lauren and Eleanor were capable, self-directed, and busy, interested in being independent and doing their schoolwork with gusto. Roseanne kept her feelings to herself, perhaps in response to her difficult family life. Chi-Ju did not speak English very well, and expended her interpersonal energies trying to build friendships with her peers, not with me. I did not push myself on these children. A loving response to their indifference is to accept it at face value and remain open to the possibility of a relationship developing in the future.

And then there were the children I had trouble liking. This was always a difficult one: if I am committed to loving each of my students, how do I handle the children whom I find unappealing? In some cases—Andy, for example—time and perseverance might lead to a solution. Andy was a whiner. He was mean to the other children, and had a paralyzingly negative attitude. No matter which activity he was assigned to, he would groan. He started every task, regardless of what it was, by sitting down and saying "I hate this . . . do I have to do this . . . ?" I tried giving him the benefit of the doubt, cutting him slack, giving him space. Then I ran out of ideas.

His negativism was contagious: once he started complaining, the other children working near him would start doing it too. I tried to diffuse the situation with humor whenever it arose—since once Andy was laughing he forgot to be miserable. And then it dawned on me. Andy didn't really hate everything, and he didn't really mind doing the work he was assigned. Being grouchy was his "shtick"; it was the only way he knew how to enter a situation. I saw Andy in a new light, and was able to ignore his complaints and help him get settled into each new project. I don't know if my interpretation of Andy's bad attitude is correct or not, but it enabled me to find a way to interact with him that would be positive and allowed me to establish a relationship with him.

Other cases were not so easy to solve. Gus, for example, was a socially immature kindergartner with fairly advanced verbal skills. At first I found him intriguing. After I had spent a few days in the corner of the classroom writing furiously in my notebook and speaking to no one, Gus came up to me. "Excuse me," he said. I looked up from my notebook. "If you have any questions, or would like me to tell you anything, anything at all, you just let me know. We can talk back and forth . . ." he offered, gesturing with his tiny, pale hands to illustrate the kind of interaction he envisioned. I nodded and tried hard not to laugh at his offer.

As I became more involved in the life of the classroom, I found Gus less and less amusing. He did his very best to shirk all his academic requirements, and would lie about having completed his work. He would torment any child he thought he had a chance of defeating: he would tease, insult, and bully. And, inevitably, he was the first to run to a teacher to tattle on other children. When Martha spoke with his mother about these issues at their parent-teacher conference, Frances replied, "I know. He's like that at home. The other day he wanted me to read to him and he said, 'Fran (idiot), please read to me.' He said 'idiot' under his breath, as if I couldn't hear it. When I told him that I didn't want to spend time with a boy who would call me names, he denied having done it."

How could I find a way to love a child like that?

Reflecting on my feelings about him in my journal, I found that there was more to my problem with Gus than I thought. I realized that he was more than just a child in the class: he was an archetype. He represented the kind of kid that I worried my son Sam might become. Like Gus, Sam is unusually verbal for his age. What would stop him from becoming arrogant, sneaky, and mean too? Gus was a walking embodiment of my fears for the future.

This was an upsetting realization. It seemed dark, tangled, messy. And it wasn't fair to Gus, either. I did my best to avoid Gus for a while, as I struggled to come up with a plan. I decided that I would just try to treat him the way that I would want Sam to be treated if he in fact did end up like Gus. I would want Sam to be treated kindly and with respect, even if he was a little weasel who drove his classmates crazy. I tried hard to love Gus, but had only limited success.

It was hard for me to admit that I didn't love Gus. I had created an image of myself as a loving teacher, and Gus burst my bubble. On some level I had expected to be able to be all-loving, to enter every interaction with every student as one-caring (Noddings 1984). My expectations, of course, were unrealistic. Love is a complex emotion. It is not monolithic and cannot be commanded at will. Looking at this gap in my teacherly love gives insight into the experience of loving teaching. Loving teachers draw upon love to guide their practice, to inform their decisions, and to serve as a heuristic for professional behavior. All that a loving teacher can do is be committed to making the effort to love her students and provide opportunities for relationships to be established and to grow. Forcing love is foolish, misguided, insensitive, and unloving. Like a flower, love must be left to blossom on its own.

The exploration of this gap in my love for my students also tells a story about my chosen profession. Teachers of young children often become prisoners of "the hegemony of nice" (Swadener 1992). The assumption that all early childhood educators are nice to all children, all of the time and in all circumstances, is pervasive. It is a notion rooted in sexist stereotypes. Early childhood teaching has traditionally been a women's job. Women are nurturing, nice, sweet. Good girls don't complain, speak up, fight back. Because we work with the youngest children, we appear to be most firmly trapped in this stereotype. And it is often reinforced with images from real life. Think, for example, of the famous picture of Lady Diana Spencer published early in her relationship with Prince Charles. She stood demurely in the play yard of the Young England nursery school, where she worked as a teacher, with two lovely little girls, one on her hip and one at her side. Diana's eyes were cast down modestly, and the sunlight behind her created a halo of her golden hair. Could England want a nicer Princess?

Of course, the ensuing years have revealed that there are many more dimensions to Princess Diana. She is strong-willed, sexy, powerful, troubled, fun-loving: she is many things, and she is much more than nice. So, too, the professional of early childhood education is much more than nice. Though many early childhood teachers are nice people, they are also thinking beings and astute professionals. Teaching young children is challenging intellectual work, work that draws on the head as well as on the heart and hands.

❖ ❖ ❖ ❖ ❖ ❖

In previous years Martha had done a unit on family just prior to Thanksgiving. My traditional pre-Thanksgiving unit had covered similar ground: an inquiry into family history, immigration, and migration linked to the California State History-Social Science framework (1988) for second grade, and a language arts unit on houses and homes. We both felt that it was nice to talk about families prior to the celebration of such a family-centered holiday, and agreed that couching the tale of the Pilgrims and Plymouth Rock in a larger investigation of family journeys was a comfortable way to handle that difficult and complicated piece of American history. We decided to co-plan and co-teach a unit on family that would both draw on our previous experiences and provide opportunities for the development of new and creative ideas. We spoke briefly about some specific lessons and activities that we'd like to include—I suggested Tom Chapin's song, "Family Tree" (Chapin and Forster 1988), and the book *A House Is a House for Me*, by Mary Ann Hoberman (1978), and Martha suggested holding a feast of family recipes and inviting all of the children's families to attend. We agreed to meet on Saturday to plan the unit.

Much to my surprise, the unit began before Martha and I met to do our planning. On the Thursday before our scheduled planning session, Martha came up to me before morning meeting and said, "Well, let's do some family writing today. Should we start the unit?" I wondered how we could start a unit that we had not yet planned. The children were still involved in their study of the solar system, but it was winding to a close: there would be a period of overlap in which the children would be finishing their planet books and getting started on the family unit. Martha thought that it seemed like a good time to get started.

Though typical of Martha's low-key approach to classroom life, this inconspicuous beginning to the unit was not my style. Prior to the start of the unit, Martha wrote in our dialogue journal and asked, "How do you think the planning should work? How do you go about setting a course?"

I responded:

> When I plan I usually brainstorm all the possible ideas, making sure I touch on all the disciplines that I can think of. I especially like to find good songs and poems. Then I juggle all the pieces around to see which ones make sense together and which will fit into the time frame at hand. I like to make sure that there are a few focal activities—things that encapsulate the themes and important concepts of the unit—and I usually open with one and close with one. The feast is a great closer. Any ideas for an opener?

I like fanfare. I like build-up. I like to generate excitement about activities and ideas, to encourage my students to get engaged and to enhance student buy-in and commitment. I like them to be as excited about our lessons and activities as I am. But this unit began "not with a bang but a whimper" (Eliot 1971). Several days into the unit, I wondered if the children knew what was going on:

> I don't know if they feel like they are doing a unit on family or not. There are so many irons in the fire—Neptune, the family unit, the cookie unit [an interdisciplinary mathematics unit on story problems and operations]—it might be hard for them to know.
> (Field Notes 11/7/94)

Collaborative studies are often marked at the outset by difficulties in communication and the negotiation of stylistic differences. I knew that Martha and I had different approaches to teaching and instruction, and I tried to keep this in mind as our unit got underway. As the children did more and more of the activities that Martha and I had planned, the focus of the unit became clearer. We found out about our names, how they were chosen and what they mean. We each brought in a favorite family recipe to contribute to a class cookbook. We thought about ways in which we were like and unlike members of our family, both as a result of genetics and as a result of living together and sharing experiences. We drew portraits. We wrote poems about our names and made banners that represented our families using visual symbols. We read poems and sang songs; we made family trees; we mapped our family heritages with string on the world map; we interviewed an adult in our family about a journey made by a family member in the past, either a journey to the United States or to Loma Prieta. Martha and I did all of these things, too—we learned about our children and they learned about us. Our unit was in full swing.

In a dialogue journal entry written as I was just beginning to co-teach in her classroom, Martha asked me how it felt to be back in the saddle again. I responded, expanding on her metaphor: "I feel like I finally found my saddle (that took a few days and a lot of looking) and dusted it off and oiled it up. And I am sitting in it and it feels pretty good. The problem is that it's not my horse!" I struggled with issues of ownership and territorialism for most of my time in Room 4. Qualitative researchers can expect to feel like "invaders of someone else's territory" (Glesne and Peshkin 1992, 55), but I felt that there was more to the problem than endemic research anxiety. The fact that the class was *Martha's* class, not *my* class, made it difficult for me to feel like a "real" teacher.

I assumed that the problem was rooted in the situation: I did not have complete control over every aspect of the educational environment and could not feel like a teacher without it. Though Martha treated me as a partner, and was very willing to share her students, her teaching time, and her materials, I just didn't feel like an equal partner. I had anticipated some difficulty with the negotiation of territory, similar to that faced by student teachers and their cooperating teachers (see Davies 1993; Nettesheim 1993). Although we did not have the professional status differential that characterizes the student teachercooperating teacher relationship, our situation was similar in that, while I was a welcome guest in Martha's classroom, I was a guest with an agenda. Like a student teacher who must learn to be a teacher during her placement, there were a number of things I needed to accomplish while I was in Room 4, and I needed Martha's support. I had a lot at stake, and I felt that I needed to tread carefully. But there were more sides to this problem than I had anticipated.

I had first faced the problem of not feeling like a real teacher when I realized that I would have to hold in check my natural responses to classroom situations in order to blend in with the culture of Martha's classroom. And now this problem was arising again, in the context of our curriculum planning. I did not feel comfortable pushing any particular activity, or asking for more closure or more specificity. As I wrote in my journal after our first planning session:

> No matter how you slice it, it is her classroom and she had final say. . . .
> In fact, when I left, I didn't even have any notes from the session. Martha
> did the writing, right into her plan book. I suppose I could have taken
> some notes, and I actually started to, but it just felt silly—why should I
> bother to write anything down if it was all going into Martha's book.
> (Field Notes 11/6/94)

My first attempt to deal with this problem was to bring it to Martha's attention. Her response, in our dialogue journal, was an open invitation to make myself at home, professionally speaking, in her classroom:

> The bottom line is I don't feel ownership and I don't feel any sense of loss
> by sharing them [the children] with you. I feel like it is more like a gift to
> share you with them. . . (a gift for both you and them), and a gift to me
> because I value and respect your knowledge, understanding, and values
> as a teacher and I want to become a better teacher for having shared this.

I responded:

> I guess I am just really territorial, and I can't understand people who
> aren't. But if you say that you're not troubled by ownership issues, then
> I'll have to believe you. I was very aware of not pushing too hard, being
> too overbearing. (This is also my attempt to keep my. . . exuberant side in
> check. You know that I can be a real steamroller when I'm not careful.) I
> guess that next time I'll just be more direct and not worry so much about
> boundaries. I'll just act like this is really my class (if that's okay with
> you!).

Martha's response should have put the matter to rest:

> As for being territorial and trying not to push too hard—I know you,
> remember?—I may be inscrutable, but I'm not completely passive. I
> wouldn't just let you run over me. I've co-planned with lots of people.
> I'm comfortable with it so what we need to do is make you comfortable
> with it.

Though we tried, I just couldn't get comfortable with it. Our unit progressed, and I still didn't feel like a real teacher.

There are many intertwined reasons for this. First, as a guest in Room 4, I had to modify my teaching to fit into the culture of Martha's classroom. In the case of Peter and Mark's disagreement over the use of a particular book, as with Gus and Rita's mathematical sparring match, I found I often had to check my immediate, gut-level, teacherly reactions and respond to situations in a way that would be consistent with Martha's style. So although I was actually teaching during my time in Martha's classroom, the practices I engaged in weren't always natural or genuine representations of my soul as a teacher. This was also the case in our co-planning: I felt it was important to let Martha take the lead, since it was really her class.

As I have pointed out earlier in this chapter, in my experience one of the perks of being a classroom teacher is the opportunity to be involved in the creation of a community, in the development of a shared ethos, and in the development of a sense of "us-ness" among the members of the class: a phenomenon that I referred to as "tribogenesis" in my teaching journal. Again, because I was a guest in Room 4, I was not able to play the role in this process that I would have played were it my own room. The structure of elementary schooling teaches elementary teachers to be soloists, accustomed to having total control, responsibility, and ownership of the life of their classrooms (1975): it was difficult for me to feel like a teacher without them.

My role as a researcher also led to a lack of continuity that affected my feeling of professional presence. Elementary teachers arrive by 7:30 in the morning and leave hours after the official end of the school day. They are with their children all day, and in California they teach all subject areas, including art, music, and P.E. They tie shoes, open thermoses, apply Band-Aids, and wipe noses. Spending only part of the day in Martha's classroom may have relieved me of yard duty, but it also prevented me from attaining the level of deep commitment that I associate with the life of a teacher. Lilian Katz (1981) describes the scope of a teacher's functions as being fairly limited and concentrated in contrast to the scope of a mother's functions. In this situation, I was a teacher with an even more limited and concentrated scope of functions: my research design curtailed my professional responsibilities.

Further, being in an elementary classroom for only a fraction of
the day is an alien notion, an irregularity in the fabric of classroom
life. Martha's classroom experience, like that of the finest
elementary classrooms, is very organic. Each day has a holistic
rhythm, an ebbing and flowing all its own. Each day exists as an
integrated whole. There are few distinctions between content
areas or disciplines, no bells to mark the passage of time, no
parade of teachers arriving and departing to teach different
subjects. I arrived with the students at the start of the day and
entered the rhythm of the room. And on most days I departed
unnoticed. The children were generally so busy finishing up their
work and enjoying free choice time that they did not hear me
shutting down Martha's computer after I'd finished my daily
journal writing, even though it always blared out the exuberant
closing theme from the Looney Tunes cartoon series—"Th-th-th-
that's All, Folks!"it seemed to announce loudly—punctuating my
time in the classroom with an auditory exclamation point. But as
I left Room 4 and walked toward my car, past the open doors and
windows of busy, buzzing classrooms, I couldn't help feeling as if
I were playing hooky. Elementary teachers belong in their
classrooms at 11:00 in the morning, not in the school parking lot.

Finally, I was constrained by the time limitation imposed by
my research design. Being a teacher, a loving teacher, takes time.
Relationships cannot be rushed. Being in Martha's classroom from
October till Christmas break meant that I would be leaving just as
I would be hitting my stride.

There was a whole constellation of reasons that influenced my
difficulty with feeling authentic in Martha's classroom, all of
which are aspects of my own personal definition of what it means
to be a loving elementary schoolteacher. Regardless of these
problematic issues, I still needed to try, to do things that would
help me regain my sense of myself as a "real" teacher. I came at it
from all different angles. I decided that I wanted to try leading
meeting:

> When I think about really being a teacher, I think that leading meeting is
> very important for me. That is a time when I feel that the ethos of the
> classroom gets communicated and reinforced. If I don't do meeting during
> the time when we are co-teaching, will I really feel that I am teaching?
> (Field Notes 11/3/94)

Martha was happy to let me lead meeting, but it didn't change my situation. So I tried again, and I decided that I needed to be responsible for more prep work:

> I think that one of the reasons that I don't feel like a real teacher is because I am not involved in any of the behind-the-scenes dirty work— no preparing construction paper, no making charts, no making wall-size graph paper to be filled in by the kids, no weekly newsletter, no writing notes to parents, no ongoing anecdotal observations, etc. I think that a lot of love-energy goes into these mundane tasks, just as it goes into diaper changing, making big bowls of Flintstones macaroni and cheese for Sam, feeding watery rice cereal to Noah's inexperienced but hungry mouth. I can ask Martha to allow me to take more responsibility for these things, I guess. But it just doesn't feel 100% right because it is not my real classroom. . . .
> (Field Notes 11/8/94)

Martha was happy to let me do some of the prep work. But no matter what I tried, I had trouble feeling "real."

The family unit ended on the day before Thanksgiving break. The unit had blossomed into something very clear and visible to the students. They had experiences with family in almost every content area: language arts, social studies, math, science, music, the arts. They had experiences in almost every mode of representation: painting, music, poetry, drama. Our culminating activity was a Feast of Family Recipes, held in the last hours of school on Wednesday, just prior to vacation. Each child had brought in a favorite recipe to add to a class cookbook; parents brought a sample of their dish to the feast for all to share. The room was bursting with the fruits of the children's thinking, learning, creating, and hard work. Poetry charts, a listening station with a tape of the children reading their family journey stories, class books, handmade placemats, family portraits, maps, photographs: seeing the children's work made the unit look substantial, impressive.

The morning of the feast was a busy time. The children were bustling around, working to get the room ready before our guests arrived. Martha and I had a few activities planned, but most of the children preferred to make decorations for the feast. Sophie drew a crowd. She was making a welcoming sign—"welcome to are thasgiving fyst," it said—on a large piece of easel paper. A group of children pulled up a circle of chairs around her, watching and making suggestions. The atmosphere was warm, comfortable, and cozy. It felt almost magical, golden. The kids had clicked, and had come together as a group. On this day they were no longer twenty-four individual children in the same class, they were a class. And for me, passion, commitment, and intimacy had finally coalesced.

This morning was special for Martha, too. During one of our conversations I asked her when she felt best as a teacher, and the feast morning was the first thing she mentioned:

> There's lots of times when I feel really good, but I don't know if it's necessarily about being a teacher. I don't know, I guess on Wednesday, I felt really nice, especially . . . (pause) their excitement. Even some of the stuff that they took on on Wednesday to do, like making the signs and all that stuff that came out of (pause) that they wanted to do it, they were so engaged in doing it. And just, as a group, their enthusiasm as a group on Wednesday.

Moments like these are precious for teachers. I felt proud. Our unit had been a success. When we planned the unit, I had hoped that it would both be about family and also serve to build a feeling of family in the class. The tenor of the room that morning was proof that it had happened.

❖ ❖ ❖ ❖ ❖ ❖

The introductory letter that I sent to the parents of Martha's students before I began my fieldwork included a list of all my academic and professional credentials. Then, before describing my research plans, I casually mentioned that I was the mother of two sons, one of them two years old and the other eleven weeks old. I hoped that this would reassure any worried parents, thinking they might conclude that someone who was a mother wouldn't do any research that would harm their children. On my first day of fieldwork, one of the students' mothers came up to me and said "Hi! I'm Joan, the room mother. And you must be The Wonder Mom! *How* do you do it?"

I didn't have an answer, and it took all of my resolve to hold back the tears. The challenge of being both a mother and a teacher of young children felt enormous. As I sat in Martha's classroom, I often yearned to be with my young sons, struggling with what Dorothy Smith (1987, 6) calls the problem of "bifurcated consciousness." I felt deeply troubled by the irony that other women were watching them so that I could sit in a classroom and watch other women's children (see Grumet 1988). I tried hard to love the children of these other women, just as I hoped that my sons' teachers were trying hard to love them. Would it be possible?

Chris Zajac (Kidder 1989, 159) arrived at a solution that worked for her: she reserved the word *love* for use with her own children. She felt that this enabled her to "keep her feelings and responsibilities in proper order." She also felt that "she was a better, more objective teacher since having her own children." Clearly this was not going to work for me: I had no desire to be a more objective teacher. And as for keeping responsibilities in their proper order, I did not worry that the students were deflecting my energies from my own children. I was experiencing just the opposite: it seemed like my children were interfering with my ability to attend properly to my students. Wrestling with this sense of conflicted loyalties, one of the essential contradictions of being a mother and a teacher, was a recurring issue throughout my fieldwork.

An example: Carlos and Dara and Peter and I sat at the zigzag table. We were all bent over our work. We had just read *A House Is a House for Me* (1978), a delightful rhyming book built around the theme of a house metaphor: "A glove is a house for a hand, a hand; a stocking's a house for a knee. A shoe or a boot is a house for a foot and a house is a house for me!" We were innovating the text, making up our own "house is a house" metaphors. Images from my everyday life sprang quickly to mind. "Pajamas are a house for a toddler," I wrote, with the memory of my struggle to get Sam out of his pajamas that morning still fresh in my mind. A garbage can is a house for Oscar the Grouch, my heart is a house for my baby. My breast is a house for milk. A family is a house for love. These issues were never far below the surface of my life in Martha's classroom.

During Thanksgiving weekend my sons were napping and I sat down at the computer to reflect on our own Thanksgiving feast. I had been trying to make sense of my conflicted feelings. Did I love Martha's students?

November 25—weekend reflections

I had what feels like a big realization: motherlove and teacherlove aren't the same thing. Duh, right? But this set off my thinking in a big way.

I have been feeling that I don't love Martha's kids. But I think it's because my idea of what it means to love kids has been changed by motherhood. When I was teaching at Grote I felt strong, loving feelings for my students. I believe that this was teacherlove. And then I left the classroom, went to grad school and had two kids. Leaving the classroom to go to grad school caused my experience of teacherlove to fade slightly over time: I clearly remembered that I had felt it, but the feelings were not at my fingertips.

Having my own children dramatically changed my notion of what it means to love children. Now I was feeling motherlove.

So when I began my research, I had not been in a classroom with kids for almost four years—my sense of teacherlove and how it feels faded, eclipsed totally by motherlove. When I went into Martha's classroom, then, I felt like I felt nothing because I didn't feel for Martha's kids the way I feel for Noah and Sam. But of course I don't! Motherlove and teacherlove are two different things. Motherlove is passion-filled and deep and personal and tangled. . . . Teacherlove is more general, reasonable, neutral, whatever. . .

Because my sense of what it means to love children was transformed by my time out of the classroom and the birth of my sons, I was looking for the wrong thing. I was waiting to feel love for Martha's kids, but I kinda expected to feel for them the way I feel for my own children, and this never happened. So I worried that I didn't feel any love for them at all. But now I realize that I do love them. It's just not motherlove that I feel for them, it's teacherlove. So on Wednesday when we were all wearing our turkey helmets and laughing our fool heads off, what I felt WAS love—it was teacherlove. And when Amy sat on the sofa "reading" *The Doorbell Rang* to herself (and then to Carlos), calling back to me if she needed help with a word, the pride and excitement and warmth and happiness I felt WAS love—it was teacherlove.

I had been making the mistake of expecting that I'd feel for them what/how I feel for my own kids. No way! That's not possible, reasonable, appropriate, or necessary. So I thought that I didn't love them. But I do—it's just a different kind of love.
(Field Notes 11/25/94)

I had arrived at a solution. Though it may seem like a simple semantic distinction, I felt it clarified everything.

Not long after I had my revelation about motherly love and teacherly love I began to feel like a "real" teacher. I had moved into the portion of my study during which I was supposed to phase myself out of active participation in the classroom. But I couldn't. I tried to be just a classroom helper, like the volunteer mothers who work in the classroom.    But there was more to it, much more.  In my journal I wrote:

> Today I was just a helper in terms of responsibilities and planning,.  But I felt like much more than that in terms of my investment in the kids and their experience, and in my commitment to helping them do the best work that they could.  I also felt that they looked to me as a real (official? authorized?) source of information and guidance, asking questions like "Lisa G.!  Where do we put this?"  and "Lisa G., now what?  I finished my chain, what do I do next?"  In fact, someone was surprised when they asked me how to attach the cityscape to the calendar and I said that I didn't know how, that they had to ask Martha.  The kid said "What do you mean you don't know?  Aren't you a teacher?"  That made me feel great— I was really a part of it.
>  (Field Notes 11/29/92)

But the real proof follows:

> There were visitors in the classroom today, people who came to look at Bayview.  (This happens with almost alarming frequency.)  I actually caught myself wondering for a moment whether they thought that I was the teacher.  And I kinda hoped that they did.  Not to take anything away from Martha, of course, but just because being a teacher feels so nice.  And because I kinda feel like these kids' teacher.
> (Field Notes 11/29/92)

Issues of territory and control, of leading meeting and doing prep work were a part of my sense of myself as a "real" teacher. But my realization that I was feeling a kind of love for the children in the class also contributed to my feelings of professional authenticity.  Teacherly love is a distinct set of feelings, the presence of which is an integral part of my professional identity.

I got a telephone call from Martha the night before my last day of fieldwork.  This was one of the many, many telephone conversations we exchanged during the period of my fieldwork. We could talk about each day's experience in the classroom for hours. And, often, we did.

"I was thinking about tomorrow," Martha said.  "I'm just not ready for you to leave.  And I'm not the only one.  Chihoe was kissing your picture today after you left."

✧ ✧ ✧ ✧ ✧ ✧

When we finished our family unit, Martha moved on to a unit on night, stars, and solstice. The culminating activity was an in-class pajama party, held on my last day in the classroom. Stars and moons hung from the ceiling. The curtains were drawn, and tiny white Christmas lights that Martha had hung up twinkled overhead like stars. We all wore our pajamas, our bathrobes, and our slippers. We listened to lullabies, put on shadow puppet shows, and read stories. It was an intimate time, a private time. Families were not invited, the classroom volunteers were given the morning off. It was just us: Martha, our kids, and me. Peter had on his pajamas: a Bill Clinton T-shirt and long johns with big ladybugs all over them. Chihoe's pjs looked like a red flannel business suit, albeit one covered with dalmatians. Martha didn't have a nightgown, so she wore one of mine. It billowed around her like an enormous sail as she floated around the classroom helping the children make their hot chocolate and french toast. Catherine, a kindergartner who had not uttered more than five words during my time in the classroom, came up to me and said, "I know new song. It called Jingle Bell. Want to hear it, Lisa G.?" And she sang at the top of her lungs: "Jingle, bell, jingle bell, jingle oh the way. Oh wah wah wah, wah wah wah wah, mumblemumblemumblemumble slay-o!" Mark flopped onto the couch and said, to no one in particular, "This is the best day of my life!"

That's when I started to cry. I took off my pajamas, picked up my briefcase, and went to pick up Sam and Noah at day care.

# 4

# Mothers and Teachers

In her powerful and influential book on the experience of motherhood, *Of Woman Born*, Adrienne Rich pointed out that "we know more about the air we breathe, the seas we travel, than about the nature and meaning of motherhood" (1976, 11). Exploring the nature and meaning of mothering is an important step in understanding teaching with love. A child's first experience with loving teaching—good or bad—generally takes place in earliest childhood, in the home, with his or her mother. This fact, coupled with the lack of careful analysis of the distinctions between motherly love and teacherly love, leads to cloudy and complicated relationships between mothers and their children's teachers.

Both Martha and I confronted the challenges inherent in these cloudy and complicated relationships during the course of this study. Martha found herself locked in conflict with many of the mothers of her students. Tensions, though generally unspoken, ran high. Something about the nature of Martha's teaching raised uncomfortable questions for the parents, for Martha herself, and for me as a researcher. What are the appropriate and acceptable boundaries of teacherly love and motherly love? Is there room for both in the lives of young children? Is school the right place for love? And what of the experiences of women like myself, who are both teachers and mothers? Is it possible to balance the complementary and contradictory responsibilities of motherly love and teacherly love?

Questions like these send me hurrying back to the ethic of care and the feminist theoretical foundations of this study. One of the central regions of women's experience explored and examined in feminist moral theory is motherhood and the act of mothering. Virginia Held (1987), for example, points out that the model of human relationship that has been seen as the paradigm of traditional moral theory, the marketplace image of buyer and seller arriving at a mutually satisfactory agreement, does not accurately represent the most basic and essential form of human interaction. In its place she suggests the mother-child relationship as the paradigm for human interaction. In this model, conflict and competition are replaced by trust and cooperation. Reshaping moral theory in this light puts care and concern at the center of moral experience.

Held discusses the nature of the mothering relationship and explores its power. Though not all women are mothers, all women are potential mothers. Every woman needs to grapple with a fundamental decision: to give birth to children or to forgo giving birth to children. And once a woman decides to give birth, pregnancy puts her in a uniquely powerful position. Held writes:

> It is women who give birth to other persons. Women are responsible for the existence of new persons in ways far more fundamental than men. It is not bizarre to recognize that women can, through abortion or suicide, choose not to give birth. A woman can be aware of the possibility that she can act to prevent a new person from existing, and can be aware that if this new person exists, it is because of what she has done and made possible. (1987, 121)

A mother bears this deep and personal responsibility for the life of her child.

Held also speaks about the impact of the process of childbirth on the mother's feelings of relation to the child: "In giving birth, women suffer severe pain for the sake of new life. Having suffered for the child in giving the child life, women may have a natural tendency to value what they have endured pain for. . . . The suffering of the mother who has given birth will more easily have been worthwhile if the child's life has value" (123). Held avoids an essentialist argument—that mothering is a purely natural instinct—by focusing on the issues of responsibility and choice. Once women have made the decision to have children and endured the process of bearing them, they are disposed to care for them.

Sara Ruddick also focuses on the experience of mothering in developing her "morality of love" (1987, 243). She suggests that there is a kind of reasoning more common to women than men, a reasoning that arises as a result of doing the work more commonly associated with women, namely, mothering. As already mentioned in Chapter One, Ruddick calls this type of moral reasoning "maternal thinking" (1989). She describes it as an intellectual discipline:

> I speak about a mother's thought—the intellectual capacities she develops, the judgements she makes, the metaphysical attitudes she assumes, the values she affirms. Like a scientist writing up her experiment, like a critic working over a text, or a historian assessing documents, a mother caring for children engages in a discipline. She asks certain questions—those relevant to her aims—rather than others; she accepts certain criteria for truth, adequacy, and relevance of proposed answers; and she cares about the findings she makes and can act on. (1989, 24)

Ruddick does not shy away from issues of gender difference—maternal thinking is a particular way of interacting with the world that is most commonly associated with women—but resists essentialism by asserting that maternal thinking can be done by men or women: a mother is "a person who takes on responsibility for children's lives and for whom providing child care is a significant part of her or his working life" (Ruddick 1989, 40).

The nature of mother's work makes maternal thinking a feminist standpoint. Drawing from the work of Nancy Hartsock, Ruddick explains:

> A standpoint is an engaged vision of the world opposed to and superior to dominant ways of thinking. As a proletarian standpoint is a superior vision produced by the experience and the oppressive conditions of labor, a feminist standpoint is a superior vision produced by the political conditions and distinctive work of women. . . . By "women's work"—the basis for a feminist standpoint—Hartsock has in mind "caring labor": birthing labor and lactation; production and preparation of food; mothering; kin work; housework; nursing; many kinds of teaching; and care of the frail elderly—all work that is characteristically performed in exploitative and oppressive circumstances. (1989, 129–30)

The discipline of mothering, then, has a political as well as an epistemological dimension. Maternal thinking is more than mommies being nice to their children. It is a way of looking at and interacting with the world that is rooted in the domestic sphere but has implications for life in the broader arena of moral life.

The central tenet of Ruddick's position is that maternal thinking is rooted in, and specific to, the lived experience of mothers. Engaging in "caring labor" and working to protect the life and foster the growth of children is the foundation for this way of thinking. Responses of care predominate in maternal practices; maternal thinking is rooted in maternal practice.

Like Ruddick, Nel Noddings (1984) draws upon the mother's experience of caring as a foundation of ethical behavior. Though not everyone will be a mother, or can be a mother, everyone has had a mother, and, as a result, has had the experience of being cared for. It is experience with caring relations that sets the stage for her perspective on caring, described in detail in Chapter One.

Feminist moral theory and the ethic of care are closely linked to motherhood and mothering. But what does it mean to be a mother? What are the dimensions of mothering? Motherhood is a complex experience, full of conflict and contradiction. Looking back on her experience as a mother in order to write *Of Woman Born*, one of the first scholarly books on the topic of motherhood, Adrienne Rich recalls:

> I knew only that I had lived through something which was considered central to the lives of women, fulfilling even in its sorrows, a key to the meaning of life; and that I could remember little except anxiety, physical weariness, anger, self-blame, boredom, and division within myself: a division made more acute by the moments of passionate love, delight in my children's spirited bodies and minds, amazement at how they went on loving me in spite of my failures to love them wholly and selflessly. (1976, 15)

Motherhood was not the subject of careful scholarly scrutiny until the mid-1970s. The images of motherhood which had dominated our thinking up until that point (and which are still very prevalent today) tended to take the form of bipolar opposites. For example, Thurer (1994) describes the two mythic mothers, the Madonna and the Witch; Swigart (1991, 5) writes of the belief that "women were either good mothers who made their children happy or bad mothers who made them miserable." Freudian psychology, the popular media, Western religion, and many other factors have worked in concert to obscure and conceal the experiences of mothering.

When mothering and motherhood are visible topics for research, the literature reflects the contradictory nature of mothering. It ranges widely, covering the gamut from the idealization of motherhood and the motherhood mystique (Fraiberg 1977, among many others) to the condemnation of motherhood as the prime location of patriarchal oppression and a call for its immediate elimination (Firestone 1970; Allen 1982). Mothers are blamed and celebrated, damned and praised, sometimes in the same breath.

The myth of the good mother has a hegemonic quality in White western culture (Glenn 1994). It is profoundly pervasive. Advertisements featuring smiling, fulfilled mommies, advice from child-rearing experts, and the cultural residue of a generation of television mothers promulgate this myth, which Rich (1976, 25) refers to as "the mask of motherhood." The myth is both alluring and repulsive, and it is simultaneously impossible to attain and difficult to resist. This leads mothers into a terrible dilemma. Thurer describes the paradox beautifully:

> What we have today is a myth of motherhood that defies common sense. Never before have the stakes of motherhood been so high—the very mental health of the children. Yet, never before has the task been so difficult, so labor intensive, subtle, and unclear. At the very moment when women have been socialized into wanting something more than a diaper in one hand and a dust rag in the other, they are obliged to subordinate their personal objectives by an ideology that insists that unless they do, they will damage their children for life. (1994, xxiii–xxiv)

Many feminist writers have taken a hard look at motherhood and have found it wanting. The major works on this subject—by Nancy Chodorow (1978), Adrienne Rich (1976), and Dorothy Dinnerstein (1976)—share the belief that the institution and experience of motherhood is the root of oppression and a source for the reproduction of gender inequality. Some suggest that any woman who chooses to stay home to raise her children is supporting the patriarchy (Dixon 1991). Jeffner Allen (1982, 315), for example, states that "motherhood is dangerous to women" as it severely curtails our freedom and keeps us subjugated.

The myth of the good mother and the feminist response are fairly stark contrasts. Research suggests that the reality of mothering is not so stark, neither black nor white but somewhere in the middle, and that many women's realities often swing through the gray areas between these two extremes (sometimes even in the same morning). Again and again (Bernard 1975; Boulton 1983; Burck 1986; Dally 1982; Friedland and Kort 1981; Hoffnung 1989; Holland 1980; Lazarre 1976; Minturn and Lambert 1964, among many others), research reports that motherhood is an experience fraught with ambivalence (Ruddick 1987), an experience both joyous and oppressive (Rossiter 1988). It can be incredibly rewarding, but also incredibly difficult.

The act of birthing and raising children is challenging, to be sure, but motherhood also has an impact on women's sense of self and their status in society. Thurer points out that

> . . . even as mother is all-powerful, she ceases to exist. She exists bodily, of course, but her needs as a person become null and void. On delivering a child, a woman becomes a factotum, a life support system. Her personal desires either evaporate or metamorphose so that they are identical with those of her infant. Once she attains motherhood, a woman must hand in her point of view. (1994, xvii)

Thurer's ironic spin on the situation highlights the one of the many enormous repercussions of becoming a mother: women lose their autonomy, deeply involved in a relation that lasts two lifetimes.

One morning, as I sat in Martha's classroom, I had the opportunity to see the unsightly banner of mothering unfurl before my eyes. Connor sat working beside his mom. She was volunteering in the classroom that day, and was sitting at a table helping children with a writing assignment. Connor struggles with a handful of severe learning difficulties, and his mother has struggled beside him every step of the way. His battles are her battles. She shares his victories and his defeats. As she leaned over his work to offer encouragement and advice, Connor lashed out, hitting her several times on the arms and torso. The other children looked up from their work, shocked. They had never seen Connor get that angry, and they had never seen anyone hit his or her mother at school. They stared at Connor and his mom, waiting to see what would happen. They waited. I waited. But nothing happened. Connor returns to his work. His mom, sighing, turns to assist another student. To me-the-teacher this interaction was shocking and bewildering. But to me-the-mother it made perfect sense.

Connor and his mother represent one face of motherly love. It is intense and deep, distinctly intimate and personal but, oddly, not at all private. Most mothers would acknowledge its existence and its importance in their lives, and the dramas of motherly love are often enacted in public settings: the checkout line at the supermarket, the mall, the playground, the school.

It is important to note that when I use the term motherly love, I am not referring to maternal instinct. Maternal instinct is widely considered to be an essentialist myth, a result of cultural conditioning and socialization rather than an innate drive (Rich 1976; Chodorow 1978; Badinter 1981; Dinnerstein 1976; and many others). Motherly love is a feeling, or a set of feelings, linked to a relationship. It is also important to note that my understanding of motherly love is rooted in my own experience as a mother, and as a result, like most of the writings on the subject, it reflects a late twentieth century, white, Western, middle class, college educated perspective. Studies of mothering in African American, Native American, Hispanic, and Asian American cultural contexts (see essays in Glenn, Chang, and Forcey 1994; Collins 1991); historical studies (Aries 1962; Thurer 1994); international studies (Kitzinger 1979; Minturn and Lambert 1964); and studies of mothers in poverty (Polakow 1993) tell other stories of mothers, mothering, and motherly love.

The literature on motherly love as it plays out in white Western culture tells a story of simultaneous joy and anger, a story of "a fiercely passionate love that is not destroyed by the ambivalence and anger it includes" (Ruddick 1989, 29). No scientific studies have been done to explore the phenomenon of motherly love (Sternberg 1988b): studies of mothers and their children focus on more concrete and observable behaviors like attachment (Ainsworth 1978; Bowlby 1966) and physical contact (Harlow 1986). Instead, the literature on the experience of mothering and the nature of motherly love is ripe with mothers' stories, the kind of compelling stories that have the power to bring tears of recognition to the eyes of mother readers. For example, Adrienne Rich writes:

> But, having borne three sons, I found myself living, at the deepest levels of passion and confusion, with three small bodies, soon three persons, whose care I often felt was eating away at my life, but whose beauty, humor, and physical affection were amazing to me. I saw them not as "sons" and potential inheritors of patriarchy, but as the sweet flesh of infants, the delicate insistency of exploring bodies, the purity of concentration, grief, or joy which exists undiluted in young children, dipping into which connected me with long-forgotten zones in myself. I

was a restless, impatient, tired, inconsistent mother, the shock of
motherhood left me reeling; but I knew I passionately loved those three
young beings. (1976, 194)

This maternal ambivalence seems to lead inexorably to guilt.
Psychologist Shari Thurer (1994, xi) writes that she "cannot recall
ever treating a mother who did not harbor shameful secrets about
how her behavior or feelings damaged her children." There is "a
physical and psychic weight of responsibility" (Rich 1976, 52) on
mothers that can be overwhelming. Often mothers turn to books
written by child-rearing experts to try to ensure that they are
doing right by their children, but this often makes matters worse
(Grieshaber 1996; Marshall 1991; Phoenix and Woollet 1991). As
Thurer points out:

Exactly how does mom proceed to "enjoy" the baby who is spitting out
food, mashing it into every crevice in reach, and throwing it in her face?
While child care specialists intend to reassure mothers, in fact they often
foster a nagging sense of bewilderment, wrongdoing, and guilt. In effect,
they have invented a motherhood that excluded the experience of the
mother. (1994, xiii)

Knowledge about the universality of guilt and anxiety in
motherhood did little to assuage my own conflicted feelings
around working on this study. In my fieldwork journal, just a few
lines after my realization about the distinction between
"motherlove" and "teacherlove," I wrote:

It drives me crazy to be sitting here at the computer, writing about loving
kids and ignoring my own. Sam has been walking up and down the hall
outside my door, plaintively asking, "Mommy, where are you?" He has
asked it so many times that it has transformed itself into a little game.
Now he prances along and chants a sing-song "Mommy? Where are
you? Mommy? Where are you?" over and over. Noah rustles in his
crib, waking from a nap and requesting a nursing. What the fuck am I
doing here?
(Field Notes 11/25/94)

I typed these words feverishly, trying to get all my thoughts
down on paper before Sam lost interest in prancing and chanting,
and before Noah's needs became too insistent: I rushed to finish
my work before the pressing responsibilities of motherhood
became too urgent to ignore. I felt torn—I was angry at my kids

for taking me from my work, and I was angry at my work for taking me from my kids.

I often felt that no mother struggled with this conflict as I did. But, as the feminists of the 1970s taught us, the personal is political: my experience is shared widely by many mothers (Lightfoot 1978). As I read more deeply on the subject of mothers' struggles to make room for their professional selves and their mothering selves, these same kinds of conflicted feelings surfaced again and again. Adrienne Rich (1976, 279) reprints a poem by the poet Alta that deals honestly with this conflict, and which conveys so much more than expository prose can ever capture. I felt as if I could have written these words myself:

> a child with untameable curly hair. i call her kia,
> pine nut person, & her eyes so open as she watches me try
> to capture her,
> as I try to
> name her . . .

> what of yesterday when she chased the baby in my room
>         and i screamed
> OUT OUT GET OUT & she ran
> right out but the baby stayed
> unafraid. what is it like to have
> a child afraid of you, your own
> child, your
> first child, the one . . .

> who must forgive you if either of you are to survive . . .
> & how right is it to shut her out of the room so i can
>         write about her?
> how human, how loving, how can
> i even try to
> : name her

> maybe they could manage w/out me
> maybe I could steal
> away a little time
> in a different room
> would they all still love me
> when i came back?

As I engaged in this study, I grappled with two categories of discomfort, intertwined and overlapping, regarding the relationship between my work in schools and my work with my sons. The tensions I faced as I juggled research/writing and mothering, captured so vividly in Alta's verse, existed in tandem with the tensions I faced as I juggled early childhood teaching and mothering. In this latter arena, the distinctions between motherly love and teacherly love became blurred and elastic. Motherly love and teacherly love may be different things, but what does it mean when one woman feels both? What happens when a tired and frazzled teacher leaves her students at the end of the school day and goes home to her children, children who have, perhaps, spent their day driving their own teachers to distraction? Thinking of my son Sam's contribution to my difficult feelings for Gus, I wondered if my life as a mother helps or hinders my life as a teacher (see Lightfoot 1978). Thinking about some of the professional challenges of being a teacher of young children—long hours, a salary just large enough to cover the costs of day care for my two sons, the inflexible daily schedule that does not bend, no matter how badly Noah's ear is infected—I wondered if my being a teacher enhances or detracts from my ability to be a good mother.

Does being both a teacher and a mother enable me to better understand the mothers of my students and of Martha's students? I had many opportunities to think hard about these issues, fraught as Martha's classroom life was with challenging and complicated relationships with her students' parents.[8]

Martha's undergraduate degree is in child development, not education, and she tends to think of herself as an early childhood educator rather than an elementary school teacher. NAEYC (Bredekamp 1987) defines early childhood as the period from birth through age eight, the end of second grade: Martha's K-1-2 class fits squarely within those parameters. In his influential book on schooling and the development of young children, *The Hurried Child* (1981), psychologist David Elkind encourages teachers and parents to refrain from rushing their young children through early

---

[8]Biklen (1992) points out that when teachers talk about "parents" they generally mean mothers. In the discourse of education the word parents is often used in an attempt to avoid the gender issues and conflicts that "lurk as the subtext" (157) to mother-teacher encounters. Like Biklen and the teachers she and I have worked with, I refer both to mothers and to parents but I almost always mean mothers.

childhood, and from forcing them into structured academic learning too quickly. Martha's views on the importance of process over content, her informal relationship with assessment, and her belief that children will take from any classroom activity whatever it is that they need at a given moment are well aligned with her conception of her classroom as an early childhood education setting.

This philosophical orientation, embodied in full flower in Martha's classroom, is very much in keeping with Bayview School's stated mission. And the children at Bayview are there because their parents have made the choice to send them there. Despite this, some of the parents of Martha's students were concerned about what their children were experiencing, and at times their worries were communicated to Martha in backhanded ways. One mother laughed nervously and told Martha that her child had said that they never do any work at school. Another made a comment about her child only bringing home art projects in her work folder, and no "real work." Other parents were more direct. One mother told Martha that at the end of last year her daughter was able to add with regrouping and now she couldn't. She had concluded that it was because Martha's program didn't include any mathematics that her daughter was losing all of her skills. Parents of kinders worried that the work was too hard; parents of second graders worried that the work was too easy. It seemed as if no one was happy.

Martha was not sure how to respond. The parents' criticism made her feel insecure and angry. She knew that she was providing a safe, challenging, and engaging educational environment for the children. She knew that a great deal of research supported her program. She knew that she had been hired by Bayview to teach exactly as she was teaching. She suspected that the parents' comments stemmed from a lack of knowledge about child-directed, experiential education coupled with the high level of anxiety that characterized parental life in the high-achieving town of Loma Prieta, and she hoped that the comments were not meant to be personal attacks. But she found herself getting up in the morning and thinking, "Oh God, I don't want to go to work! I don't want to go, I don't want to go!" The stress of parent pressure made her doubt herself and her skills, and tempted her to throw her standards out the window. She told me, "If the parents want math worksheets, then fine, they can have them. That would be a million times easier for me to do than what I'm doing now anyway!"

Scholars have characterized the relationship between mothers and female elementary schoolteachers as hostile and conflict-ridden (Ribbens 1993; Biklen 1992; Lightfoot 1977; Lightfoot 1978; Levin 1987; among others): McPherson (1972) has called them "natural enemies." Mothers and their children's teachers share a great deal of territory as a result of their gendered relationship to children, and are (often unacknowledged) partners in the struggle to reverse the devaluation of the work associated with raising and educating young children. Biklen (1992, 155) asserts that mothers and teachers tend to overlook their commonalities, and instead "resist traditional images of domesticity through conflict with each other, the teachers by resisting mothers' demands and the mothers by attempting to insert their knowledge into the pedagogical arena." Similarly, Lightfoot (1977, 404) argues that "mothers and teachers are caught in a struggle that reflects the devaluation of both roles in this society." Martha and her difficult mothers were playing out a drama that has been well documented: her classroom became "a site where women struggle with each other for status and control" (Biklen 1992, 170).

Martha never compromised her standards by passing out math worksheets, and the parent community calmed down somewhat over time. Parent conferences helped a great deal: many of the most skeptical parents were surprised to find out how much Martha knew about their children, how able she was to talk about their growth and their learning, how much she cared about them as individuals. Parents were also able to get a sense of perspective by spending time in Martha's classroom. The children's parents are welcome to volunteer in the room at any time, and many of them do; Martha has a roster of more than 13 regular volunteers who work in the classroom each week. At first it seemed to Martha almost as if some of the mothers were coming in as spies, checking up on her teaching and examining the work being done, then reporting back to the underground parent network. But this too relaxed over time, and many of the spies became transformed into supporters. But conflict and tension with the parent community has continued to be a struggle for Martha in her work at Bayview.

In an attempt to find out if my own life as a mother gave me an insider's understanding of this difficult situation, I tried to make sense of the behavior of these mothers. Many of the things they were criticizing in Martha's teaching practices and philosophy were an explicit part of the Bayview School mission. These parents had elected to enroll their children in Bayview, a school with a clear and explicit philosophy, yet seemed angry and frustrated by the operationalization of that philosophy.

Perhaps these parents were eager to enroll their children in Bayview simply because it is the thing to do: I suspect that many parents enter the admissions lottery just because they have heard good things about Bayview, but have no real idea of what the school is all about. And once they have won a highly coveted spot for their child, why give it up? If so many people want it, it must be worth having! Children can always be pulled out and sent back to their neighborhood school if things don't work out.

Perhaps the parents were putting Martha through some kind of hazing ritual, a trial by fire for the new teacher. Or perhaps they still felt some kind of loyalty to the teacher whom Martha replaced. Her predecessor had been at Bayview since its inception over 20 years ago, and was a very beloved member of the community. She retired, stricken with breast cancer. Many of the second graders in Martha's class had been first graders in that classroom the previous year; even now, they still meet some of Martha's suggestions with, "We didn't do it that way last year!"

Or perhaps it had something to do with Martha herself. Perhaps the parents felt threatened somehow. In many ways, Martha's teaching resembles good parenting, the kind to which we all aspire. She juggles the competing needs of many children with ease. She disciplines gracefully and in a consistently positive fashion. She never yells. She scaffolds the children as they reach for new heights. And she loves them.

But Martha's love for the children has a character very different from a mother's love. It is clean, neutral, unencumbered. She loves the children, but they are still quite separate from her. And at the end of their time in her classroom, she lets them go. Her love is finite in duration and scope (Katz 1981). Though this may simply be a result of Martha's reserved personality, I think it provides some insight into the nature of teacherly love. A mother's love, unlike a teacher's, is infinite. And further, as Sara Ruddick says, "Maternal love . . . is said to be gentle and unconditional when, in fact, it is erotic, inseparable from anger, fierce, and fraught with ambivalence" (1987, 246).    Unlike Martha's teacherly love,  motherly love is tangled, deep, intense, complicated, as the story of Connor and his mother so graphically illustrated.

Martha shies away from the word love in talking about her teaching practices in order to sidestep a sensitive issue, and to avoid competition and conflict with her students' mothers.  In our dialogue journal, Martha explored this further:   "I do think parents want teachers to truly like their children, know their children and care about their children—is this love—maybe, but I don't think parents would call it that."  She even went as far as to suggest that parents might not want a teacher to love their child. Despite my insider's perspective on the mother-teacher relationship, I found this somewhat puzzling.  Any one of these parents would go out of her way to hire a loving baby-sitter, au pair, or nanny for their child.  Why wouldn't they want a loving teacher?  Martha responds:

> I think fears of abuse come into it.  Also their own experience with school and teachers as children might dictate a lot of their thinking about what schooling should be.  Some parents may see teachers as a threat—it is for some the first time they've turned their children over with the expectation that they'll be strongly influenced by another adult—the academic realm is safe but the emotional realm creates perhaps a loyalty/disloyalty competitiveness.  Also perhaps because of the "authority" or "professional" role the teacher plays—some see letting emotions get involved as unprofessional.  Others may feel that teachers need to be objective quantifiers about their child's performance. . . . Also maybe parents want their child not to be so emotionally involved with teacher as teacher may serve as person to blame, shift the burden to, when children have trouble.

Madeleine Grumet (1988) explores similar territory, writing about the uneasy relationship between mothers and teachers. Mothers labor and love at home, raising their children.  Then they bring their children to school.  The children are freed from the small and private world of their home by their female elementary teachers, and released by them from their dependence on their mothers.  Grumet asserts that teachers teach children the language of the fathers and prepare them for life in the world of men.  As a result, she suggests that mothers see elementary teachers—women who take children on the journey from the domestic womanworld to the public manworld— as traitors, betraying their sex and their children, and feel contempt for them as a result.

Contempt for caring and caregiving professions is widespread in western culture. In *Moral Boundaries*, Joan Tronto discusses this phenomenon, positioning it as a political problem. "Since our society treats public accomplishment, rationality, and autonomy as worthy qualities, care is devalued insofar as it embodies their opposites . . . privacy, emotion, and the needy" (1993, 117), Tronto writes. Professions rooted in caregiving—nursing, teaching, day care, domestic work—are deemed less worthy, and have low status as a result. Tronto also asserts that the importance of caring and caring work has been degraded in order to maintain the power of those who are privileged. Because teachers do caring work, they can become objects of disdain. Martha's commitment to loving her students further complicates this situation. Traditionally, caring has belonged in the private sphere, in the home, behind closed doors. By loving children in school, a public setting, Martha crosses a boundary. Bringing care into the public domain threatens the status quo.

Lightfoot puts the uneasy alliance between mothers and teachers into a broader context. She argues that the low status of mothers and teachers makes them "perfect targets for each other's abuse. Neither dares to strike at the more powerful and controlling groups who are most responsible for their demeaning social and economic position" (1977, 404), so they lash out at each other. Unlike Grumet (1988), who believes that mothers and teachers stand in opposition to one another in terms of their relationship to "the language of the fathers," Lightfoot casts mothers and teachers as allies of a sort: they are both involved in raising children

> in the service of a dominant group whose values and goals they do not determine. In other words, mothers and teacher have to socialize their children to conform to a society that belongs to men. Within this alien context, it is almost inevitable that mothers and teachers would not feel an authentic and meaningful connection to their task and not completely value the contributions of one another. (1977, 404)

On a more personal level, mothers may also be concerned about relinquishing their omnipotent decision-making and control over the lives of their children. Gus's mother Frances approached Martha one morning with a request that illustrates this point well. Gus, a kindergartner, would be buying school lunch for the very first time that day, and Frances sheepishly requested that Martha not allow him to purchase a hot dog: Gus had never eaten a hot dog that had not been minced into tiny morsels, and, though he was five years old and physically healthy, Frances was worried that he might choke. When Martha replied that she was not with the children when they went to the lunch line and could not, and would not, influence Gus's lunch choices, tears welled up in Frances's eyes. Frances was confronted with the hard truth: that when young children enter school, for the first time in their lives day-to-day "power that has personal consequences for the child is wielded by a relative stranger" (Jackson 1968/1990, 29).

Further, mothers may feel some kind of jealousy as they relinquish their children to the teacher, who is not only another woman, but also the Other Woman (Lightfoot 1978). It might be easier for a mother to give her child over to a woman who is not loving, one who would not eclipse her in her child's stratosphere. Research suggests that many mothers define themselves first and foremost as mothers, and some even lose themselves in the mothering role (Radl 1973; Matthews and Brinley 1982). The endless demands and difficulties of mothering reinforce these women's connection with the role: it often seems to them that they do nothing else but mothering (Boulton 1983; Burck 1986). Perhaps this makes it difficult for mothers to let go of their young children, to lose them to their teachers. Further, many mothers who have chosen to make mothering their full-time career have low self-esteem (Boulton 1983; Heffner 1978; Lightfoot 1977; Radl 1973), which might make them more prone to feelings of jealousy about their children's affection for their teachers.

Widely read experts on parenting and child development (Fraiberg 1977; Bettelheim 1987; Brazelton 1969) have insisted that mothers are the people best qualified to care for children. These types of assertions add fuel to the fire of guilt and doubt that burns within many mothers. Mothers who work outside the home may feel diminished for having put their children in day care when they were preschoolers and have negative feelings about schooling as a result. Or they may feel guilty about not being able to volunteer in the classroom and chaperone field trips, for not being home with cookies and milk at the end of the school day.

Career mothers[9] may feel concerned about relinquishing the care and upbringing of their children to an inferior source.

A loving teacher like Martha complicates things, compounding the feelings of uncertainty, guilt, and doubt that are a standard feature of the "mothering discourse" (Griffith and Smith 1987, 97) and which may cloud motherhood for many women. Martha's commitment to being emotionally present for her students introduces an unexpected variable into the equation of schooling: love.

But is school the right place for love? Should love be the exclusive purview of the family? Whose responsibility is it to love children? The nature of family responsibilities versus school responsibilities is raised, in a slightly different form and context, by Lisa Delpit in her article "The Silenced Dialogue: Power and Pedagogy in Educating Other People's Children" (1988). Delpit discusses the problems inherent in many progressive, well-intentioned efforts to develop the literacy skills of African American children. She asserts that these approaches cheat these children out of their education. School should be a place, Delpit believes, where children who are not participants in the mainstream "culture of power" can learn its rules and codes. School should be explicit and direct in providing children with "discourse patterns, interactional styles, and spoken and written language codes that will allow them success in the larger society" (1988, 285). This will make it easier for those children to acquire power. Delpit quotes an African American parent as saying "My kids know how to be Black—you teach them how to be successful in the White man's world" (1988, 285). Certain specific ways of interacting with the world are taught at home; others should be taught at school. For Delpit and the parents she quotes, the boundaries are clear.

Does the same hold true for love? Is love something that belongs in the home, and only in the home? It is easy to imagine a

---

[9]I use this phrase to refer to women who have chosen to make motherhood and all it entails their work. The term "stay-at-home mother," though currently quite popular among the mothers at the playgrounds that my sons and I frequent, is too vague, too unwieldy. It is also inaccurate: if they are stay-at-home mothers, then why did they leave their homes to go to the playground? The term "full-time mother," another common job description, is problematic for me and many other mothers. It suggests that mothers who work outside the home are not mothers all of the time, as if we have time off from mothering while we are at our workplaces.

parent saying, "My job is to love this child. Your job is to teach her." In this case, as in the situation Delpit describes, the boundaries are clear. However, to contradict Delpit's scenario, nothing is lost if teachers choose to love their students. No one is hurt, cheated, or deprived. And again, despite my insider's perspective, I am left wondering about the resistance to loving students.

In order to defuse the loving feelings that characterize so many student-teacher relationships, it is necessary to give careful consideration to the nature and dimensions of teacherly love: perhaps if it were better articulated and better understood it would be less threatening and problematic. As I said in my journal entry on "motherlove" and "teacherlove," my sense of what it means to love children was altered by my experience as a mother: I had been waiting to feel for the children in Martha's class the same kind of feelings that I feel for my sons. No wonder that I doubted that I would ever be able to love Martha's students. I could not expect to feel this strongly, this intensely, about the children in Martha's class. In fact, it would be profoundly inappropriate. But teacherly love, the interpersonal face of loving teaching, is a different kind of love, one that is well-suited to the world of the classroom.

In Chapter One I discussed Lilian Katz's (1981) work on the differences between mothering and teaching. She describes seven ways in which the two part company: scope of functions, intensity of affect, spontaneity, scope of responsibility, partiality, attachment, and rationality. As I have said earlier, some of these dimensions are problematic. However, they do give some preliminary insights into the differences between motherly love and teacherly love. To extrapolate from her dimensions, it seems that motherly love is characterized by a wide scope of functions, high interpersonal intensity and strong, almost irrational attachment. Teacherly love, by contrast, is much narrower in scope, lower in interpersonal intensity, and generally weaker and more objective.

Anna Freud begins to consider the appropriate emotional territory belonging to teachers and mothers, warning that a teacher must not

> attach herself to the individual child so much as to think of him as her
> own . . . . It is only natural for her to develop strong positive feelings for
> the children on whom she spends so much of her care; she can hardly

avoid valuing, and over-valuing them, in the manner of a mother. At the same time she has to accept the necessity that her children leave her after comparatively short periods and she has to avoid rivalry with the mothers of her children. (1952, 230)

McPherson (1972, 121) also considers the emotional terrain of teaching and mothering as she contrasts the "primary" relationship of children and their parents to the "secondary" relationship of children and their teachers. Parents have particularistic expectations, focused exclusively on their own child, while teachers have more universalistic expectations, embedding the particular child in the context of the classroom. Lightfoot builds on McPherson's work, and deals directly with the comparison of parental love and teacherly love. She writes:

Nor does the teacher-child relationship suffer the chaotic fluctuation of emotions, indulgence, and impulsivity that are found in the intimate associations of parents and children. It may become a protective kind of interaction that makes it psychologically possible for teachers and children to decathect each other at the end of the year. Even those teachers who speak of "loving" their children do not really mean the boundless, all-encompassing love of mothers and fathers, but a very measured and time-limited love that allows for withdrawal. (1977, 396)

Lightfoot acknowledges the possibility of loving feelings in classroom contexts, and begins to explore their nature. They are "measured and time-limited," and have neither the depth nor breadth of parental love. Her description of motherly love as being boundless, all-encompassing, and prone to chaotic fluctuations of emotion meshes well with the current literature on motherly love, as well as with Katz's work on the differences between motherly love and teacherly love. To summarize, the research literature on this topic suggests that teacherly love can be clearly distinguished from motherly love by its limited duration and its limited intensity.

Teacherly love is certainly less expansive than motherly love; but I do not think that it is as limited as the research suggests. When Katz, for example, speaks of the limited duration of teacherly love, she is referring to limits of scope: teachers are only responsible for certain facets of a child's development, and for a circumscribed portion of each day. She does not acknowledge, however, the amount of time that many teachers spend thinking about their students outside of class time (Nias 1989; Hargreaves

1994). When the children are at risk in some way, the amount of time spent thinking, even worrying, about them is likely to increase. Caring cannot be turned on and off, as if controlled by the school bell.

The literature also overlooks one of the idiosyncrasies of teacherly love: that unlike most loving relationships, its parameters are set by the institutional calendar. Almost inevitably, when the school year ends, the children leave. Though this loss is inevitable, it is painful nonetheless: one early childhood teacher reports, "It is very hard. You feel like you're losing a part of you" (Nelson 1994, 199). All year long, teachers grow fonder and fonder of the children and are simultaneously preparing them to move on. The constant replacement of one group of loved ones by the next is an ironic phenomenon unique to teacherly love. Thus teacherly love has an unnatural rhythm, starting and stopping abruptly in response to the unfolding of the school year.

The literature may suggest otherwise, but teacherly love is also not always limited in its intensity. Caring for children, whether as a parent or as a teacher, can be demanding and exasperating. Sandra Acker (In press, 10) describes the frazzled state of a primary teacher after a particularly long day: "She loves the class, she says, though she could tear her hair out." But even after a day like this one, the teacher gets to leave the children and go home. Mothers generally do not have that option. And teachers, like mothers, are prone to perfectionism, and may face feelings of frustration and guilt when they are unable to meet fully all the needs of the children in their care (Hargreaves 1994).

Using Sternberg's (1988a) triangular theory of love to think about the relationship between motherly love and teacherly love further highlights the similarities between the two. As discussed in Chapter One, Sternberg asserts that love comprises three components: intimacy, commitment, and passion. In order to apply his model to nonsexual forms of love, I have had to modify his definitions of these components slightly, but the model is still true to its original shape and form. Intimacy represents the close, connected, and bonded feelings that characterize loving relationships. Certainly mothers have a high degree of intimacy with their children. Loving teachers, too, can experience this type of feeling toward their students, as the works which apply the ethic of care to educational settings (Noddings 1992; Martin 1992) would suggest. Commitment is straightforward, and is a crucial part of both mothering and teaching with love. Hargreaves (1994) asserts that the commitment to care is especially strong among teachers of young children. It is often a main reason they became teachers, and persists throughout their careers as a major source of job satisfaction. As Lightfoot (1977), Freud (1952), Katz (1981), and others have pointed out, though, the teacher's period of commitment and level of commitment is finite, in contrast to that of the mother.

Passion, as I have defined it, is a nonsexual energy, a drive, that compels action. Loving teachers feel passionate about their work and the lives of their classroom, and about the educational experiences of their students; mothers feel deeply passionate about their children. The passion in teacherly love is not necessarily felt for the individual students, but for learning, for the content being taught, and for the act of teaching. In contrast, the passion in motherly love is almost always focused directly on the children themselves.

These three components—intimacy, commitment, and passion—are present both in motherly love and in teacherly love, in slightly varying forms and to varying degrees. To use a metaphor to make the distinction clear, if adult-child loving relationships were to be represented as a swimming pool, then motherly love would be a lifelong swim in the deep end, while teacherly love is just a quick dip in the shallow waters. Teacherly love, like motherly love, draws on intimacy, commitment, and passion. It is different from motherlove in degree, to be sure, but it also differs in kind. Teacherlove is shaped not only by the feelings of those involved, but also by the structure of the institutions in which it occurs.

Teacherly love and motherly love are different phenomena. Though both occur within the context of young children's lives, their purposes and their very nature are deeply different. As long as the distinctions remain unexplored and unpublicized, conflict, tension, and discord between mothers and teachers is likely to continue unabated.

# 5
# Collaboration, Relationship, and Love
# in Feminist Research

As I sit at Martha's desk with my notebook in my hand, I can look to my left and see Martha's personal bulletin board. It's fairly impersonal for a personal bulletin board—it is hard to have anything really personal or private in an elementary classroom. The board has things on it like the Loma Prieta Unified School District school year calendar, Martha's class photo from last year, the Bayview faculty released time schedule, flyers from sites of potential field trips. On the chalkboard ledge, practically hidden under the edge of the teacher desk, is a photo of Martha and a smiling young man holding a tiny newborn baby. The man's arm encircles Martha's shoulders protectively, his smile somewhat tentative. Martha beams with joy, proudly holding her precious bundle. (Field Notes 10/11/94)

Martha's students love to look at that photograph. It gives them a tiny peek at a part of Martha they never get to see. They ask her questions about the photo. Who is that man? Is that your baby? Is that your house? Huh? Tell us, teacher. Share yourself with us. Please. Please? Martha answers all of their questions honestly and directly, though not with the elaborate detail the children crave. She tells them that the man is her friend Bill. The baby belongs to a friend. The photo was taken in the baby's house. I listen to these discussions silently, with a sly, smug smile on my face. I know something that Martha's students do not: the baby she holds so lovingly in the photograph is my youngest son Noah, barely twenty-four hours old when the picture was taken.

Martha George and I have been friends since 1991. We met in graduate school, when I was a first year doctoral student and Martha was a master's degree candidate on leave of absence from her teaching job. We began collaborating, and worked together extensively, because of our shared interests: we were generally the only two people in our classes interested in issues relating to early childhood and elementary education, and so we often worked together on group projects and papers. We found that we had similar values about what was important in the education of young children, and that we shared a philosophy and a vision of what schooling could be. Our academic assignments led us into collaborations of a more personal nature: we became friends.

Each of Sternberg's three components of love—intimacy, commitment, and passion—played a role in our co-teaching relationship. Given that we entered this professional alliance with a firmly established friendship, it is not surprising that the intimacy component featured most prominently in our experience. Thus, our friendship played an important role in this study. It made many things easier. Although the study was designed to explore the contributions made by care, concern, and connection to the education of young children, with its main focus on relationships between teachers and their students, it would be dishonest to ignore the relationship between the two teachers involved.

On a purely practical level, our friendship enabled me to gain easy entry into Martha's classroom. In contrast to the lengthy and difficult procedures some researchers must go through to negotiate entry—one is reminded of Alan Peshkin's (1986) experience struggling to find a fundamentalist Christian school to study—all I had to do was make a telephone call. In many ways, our friendship scaffolded me during difficult moments of the dissertation process. For example, I was able to change my plans as often as necessary—six months in your classroom; no, three months in your classroom; starting in January; no, wait, starting in October—without it feeling like an imposition. Not only was I able to bring my baby to our curriculum planning meetings, conversation sessions, and even to nurse him during many of them, but he usually spent more time in Martha's arms than my own. My transcript tapes are full of Noahsounds: gurgles and coos, squawks and cries, the ripping noise of velcro diaper covers being opened, the tinkle of his favorite rattle. We had conversations in my kitchen while my sons napped and our husbands, neglected research widowers, watched football games together.

Because Martha and I are friends, I was able to learn about events and situations that occurred in the classroom when I was not present. I heard all about Back to School Night and the ups and downs of parent-teacher conferences. If Martha received an angry telephone call from a parent, I was often the first person she would call to blow off steam. Because we were friends and trusted each other deeply, Martha felt that there was nothing about her classroom life that needed to be kept confidential. Surely most researchers do not have this kind of unlimited access.

Our level of intimacy also provided me with access of a different kind. Martha is a very reserved and private person. In one of our conversations, she revealed that she does not feel comfortable sharing her feelings or herself with people with whom she does not have a strong relationship: ". . . I don't do that with people I don't have an established caring relationship with. I just don't. It's not me. So part of me knows that I've reached that level when I'm ready to start sharing." I would not have learned as much about Martha and her teaching had we not been friends.

I felt privileged to be one of the people in Martha's inner circle of caring (Noddings 1984), but it also was a big responsibility. I needed to be sure that I did not betray her trust in me. I was delighted to be doing my research with someone with whom I already had an established relationship. But I knew that I would need to be careful not to overstep my boundaries or take unfair advantage of my insider's status. I wanted to get good data, of course, but I also wanted to remain friends with Martha when my fieldwork was over.

Our friendship and intimacy may have made certain aspects of this research endeavor easier, but our friendship also made many things harder. The literature on qualitative research indicates that these difficulties were to be expected. Glesne and Peshkin warn against engaging in "backyard studies" (1992, 21), i.e., research undertaken within one's own institution or agency, or with friends or colleagues. Backyard studies often seem like good ideas to novice researchers at first, as they involve easy access, previously established rapport, reduction in time expended, and a high degree of (perceived) utility for one's future professional life in the organization. However, being too involved in or committed to the familiar territory can lead to difficulties during the research process.

Glesne and Peshkin specifically discuss the problems of friendship within the qualitative research process, pointing to the potential for ethical conflict inherent in the fact that there are types of things that a participant might say to a friend and not to a researcher, and vice versa. Similar dilemmas are likely to arise in any research study in which the professional and the private mix.  In her study of magnet schools, Mary Hayward Metz (1986, 239) writes: "Researchers of any kind participate in a private life at the same time that they pursue a research project.  Their experiences and reflections in that private life will inevitably affect how they understand the data from their research."  Metz's understanding of her data was affected by the fact that she was a parent in the school community that she studied, with a son enrolled at one of the magnet schools she examined closely.

Some researchers avoid this problem by researching institutions or groups of people that are very different from themselves.  This phenomenon is one of the foundations of classical anthropology, captured in the image of the white scholar doing fieldwork among exotic native tribes (Malinowski 1922; Mead 1961).  It is difficult to study people just like yourself:  as you become more and more fully a true participant, you run the risk of losing the researcher's epistemological leverage.  Samuel Heilman, an Orthodox Jew who studies aspects of Orthodox Jewish life, found it very easy to enter into Talmudic study circles to do his research.  One reason for this, he posits, is that the members of the circles felt an ideological need to believe that his real reason for joining was not to do research but to fulfill the Jewish male's obligation to study Torah.  Their openness and fellowship may have made it easy for Heilman to join, but it also made his leaving that much "more painful" (Heilman 1983, 16).  He had become emotionally and intellectually involved with the members of his study circles.  This surely enhanced his work, but may also have detracted from it:  in qualitative research, as in life, every decision that reveals also conceals (Eisner 1982).

Given all this potential for difficulty, why did I bother to study the teaching of someone I know?  First, I was not able to find many teachers who were willing to state concretely that love played a role in their teaching.  And of the few I was able to find, Martha was clearly the very best teacher.  Though this study focuses on the contributions made by love to the education of young children, I felt that it was not enough for me simply to work with a loving teacher:  my teacher partner would have to be an exemplary teacher as well.  I do think that it is possible to be a good teacher without being committed to letting love play a role in your practices and your classroom.  But I also think that love alone is not enough to make one a good teacher.  I knew that if I wanted to portray loving teaching in the best possible light, I would need to work with a professional whose teaching practices would not detract from the potential impact of love in her classroom. To put it in the terms of conventional research, I wanted to hold one variable constant—excellent teaching—to allow myself to examine the other: love. As I hope Chapter Two illustrates, Martha is indeed an excellent teacher, as well as a loving one. Finally, because this study focuses on love, it seemed valuable to collaborate with someone for whom I have loving feelings: I expected that this would enhance the fidelity and consistency of the study as a whole.

This concern with fidelity and consistency springs from my commitment to positioning this study as a piece of explicitly feminist educational research. Feminist researchers have a responsibility, to quote educational philosopher R.S. Peters, to attend "to the manner as well as to the matter" (1959, 889) of our work. For example, collaboration is an essential factor in any feminist research endeavor, and it is a central issue in this study because of its focus on loving relationships in classrooms. As a result of this emphasis on caring partnership, I could not go into Martha's classroom and pretend to be an expert: both of us bring a particular combination of expertise, knowledge, and experience to bear on our shared challenge of creating and providing early childhood education rooted in love. I went into Martha's classroom as a colleague, a fellow teacher, and hoped to learn from her. Drawing on the words of scientist Cindy Cowden, who asserts that "we can only understand organisms by seeing with a loving eye" (quoted in Reinharz 1992, 3), I looked at Martha's teaching and classroom not with an enlightened eye, but with a loving one.

However, though I am a fellow teacher, I am also more than a fellow teacher. Issues of status and privilege are inherent in the collaboration of university researchers and classroom teachers. Feminist researchers may attempt to lessen the status differential between the researcher and the researched, but we can never eliminate it all together. Yes, I am a teacher, but I went into Martha's classroom not as a teacher but as a researcher, hoping to use both my emic and etic perspectives to shed light on the nature of teaching with love. As a researcher, I brought with me methods of documentation, analysis, and interpretation of practice that a classroom teacher would not ordinarily use, care about, or have time to implement in her daily professional life (Florio and Walsh 1978).

But in order to avoid the balance of power problems that often mar the research relationship, a problem referred to gently as "impositional tendencies" (Lather 1991) and strongly as "conceptual imperialism" (Stanley and Wise 1983), I designed our study to be a partnership in which both of us had something to offer and both of us had something to gain. Martha offered me the opportunity to do my research in her classroom: I had a lot to gain from that. And as a former second grade teacher in the district in which this study took place, I brought with me knowledge of the curricula and expectations of a grade level for which Martha was responsible but that she had never taught before. I also brought my teaching credential—Martha's student-teacher ratio plunged during the time I was in her classroom—so that, not only was Martha provided with a special kind of professional support during her first year in a novel teaching situation, but our endeavor offered her the opportunity to engage in the kinds of structured reflection that lead to professional growth (Florio 1984).

My vision of our teaching/research relationship as a collaborative partnership is reflected in the data gathering methods I chose and developed for this study. Interviews were replaced by two-way conversations, in which Martha and I both talked and both listened. Instead of asking Martha to write responses to my preselected prompts, we both wrote to each other in a dialogue journal. In the context of the interpretive activity, I sculpted a representation of my teaching, as did she. I was careful not to ask Martha to do something in the course of this research endeavor that I would not be willing to do myself.

And, of course, that includes teaching. The very structure of this study, with a case study and a self-study, allowed me to be more than a participant observer. I was not a voiceless, faceless, objective presence, detached and neutral. Nor was I an outsider who had managed to get the hang of the insider's ways. I lived my life in Martha's classroom as a real teacher, deeply subjective and deeply emotional, drawing on my own life experience and teacherly sense of self. Samuel Heilman (1983, 9) calls this "the native-as-stranger approach in which one turns an eye on the familiar as if it were novel and strange, taking nothing for granted while at the same time making use of the subtle understanding that only an insider can have." Heilman asserts that this method enabled him both to see action as an insider and to look into himself and explore his feelings, in order to discover the more subjective aspects of the environment. Heilman's description mirrors my intent.

In conceptualizing the specifics of my research design, I strove for consistency and fidelity: I could not think about love in classrooms and then engage in research that was not handled lovingly. Feminist methodologies—both those explicitly labelled feminist and those that are feminist in spirit—enabled me to find out more about the ways in which love contributes to the education of young children in a way that would also be consistent with my values. I attempted to operationalize the ethic of care in making each of the decisions I faced: I looked at the research as an opportunity to enter into caring relationships with others (Noddings 1984), and asked myself if the path that I was taking was one which would allow me to give care to the people with whom I would be working. In order to do this study in a way that made sense both of its feminist orientation and its location on the continuum of educational research, I found myself creating an eclectic, handmade methodology. Like a pioneer woman making a patchwork quilt, I selected the best, most appropriate swatches from my collection—swatches drawn, in this case, not from a rag bag but from recent work on teacher research, teacher biography and autobiography, and on researching one's own teaching practice, and stitched them together with feminist thread to create a finished piece that would be useful and designed to meet my specific needs and purposes. And, as with a quilt, the whole is greater than the sum of its parts.

While there is no "right" way to undertake feminist research, there is a set of issues, concerns, and practices that could be loosely grouped together and called feminist research methodologies. Feminist research methodologies grew out of feminist frustration with the inadequacies of traditional modes of inquiry. Feminist scholars are caught in a dilemma, "simultaneously immersed in and estranged from both our own particular discipline and the western intellectual tradition generally" (Westkott 1979, 422): trained to want to give an objective, reasoned account of our findings, and expected to do so, but finding ourselves faced with material that is constantly in the process of transformation (Acker, Barry, and Esseveld 1983).

Feminist researchers, tightly constrained by the structure of traditional scientific research, are caught between a rock (what feels right to us as feeling, complex human beings) and a hard place (what we have been taught is acceptable professional practice).

Just as feminist theory critiques the existing models of thought and provides an alternative which better reflects women's ways of knowing, feminist research methodologies provide guidelines for inquiry based on the fundamental assumptions and values of feminism (Smith 1987). In a statement true to feminism's assertion that the personal is political, Reinharz (1983, 162) states that "the first step in articulating a new method is to understand that one's personally experienced dissatisfaction with conventional methods is not an intrapsychic, private problem but derives from structural inconsistencies and skewed assumptions underpinning the methods themselves." Feminists thus have been compelled to create methodologies better suited to our needs.

Harding begins her critique of traditional research by examining its quest for objective knowledge. She claims that research questions are rarely requests for "so-called pure truth" (Harding 1987, 8), but are actually queries about how to change the forces at work in the world. The questions underlying feminist research, then, would ideally lead to the creation of knowledge that could be put into practice to produce changes beneficial both to women and to society in general. Women's needs, interests and experiences are the beneficiary, as well as the subject, of feminist research (Duelli Klein 1983).

Like feminism, feminist research has an explicit political agenda, and rejects the possibility of value-free knowledge. It emphasizes the worth of lived experience, and freely employs intuition, emotions, and feelings (Weiler 1985). Feminist researchers value the subjective, and deny the possibility of objective relationships between the knower and the known (Clarey, Hutchins, Powers, and Thiem 1985). Feminist research also questions the possibility of ever arriving at one "right" answer (Maher 1987), preferring instead to generate a variety of answers and stimulate further discussion and exploration.

Feminist researchers (including postmodernists and postpositivists, among others) contend that objectivity, a hallmark of traditional research, is an illusion. The scientific method is supposedly a guarantee of objective knowledge;

however, the selection of research questions, the development of methodologies, and the interpretation and discussion of findings all involve the subjectivity of the researcher (Reinharz 1992). Subjectivity is masked by the cloak of objectivity provided by the scientific method. Feminists assert that "scientific" research simply tells a story, one possible story, about the phenomena being investigated.

Feminists have also asserted that much of the problem with traditional research methods stems from the unequal balance of power in the relationship between the researcher and the subjects of the research (Messer-Davidow 1985; Harding 1987; Duelli Klein 1983; Mies 1983; Acker et al. 1983; Lather 1991). In short, "research that aims to be liberating should not in the process become only another mode of oppression" (Acker et al. 1983, 425). Feminist researchers believe that doing research "on" a woman is dehumanizing and a perpetuation of the dominant androcentric research tradition. Instead, feminist researchers prefer to do their work "for" women or "with" women (Duelli Klein 1983; Smith 1987; Lather 1991).

Drawing on Freire's (1970) notion of "conscientization," feminist researchers work to involve the subjects of their study in the process of inquiry. This can take many different forms, depending on the nature of the question and the type of research undertaken. Collaboration is a critical component in feminist research, as it is in many other forms of research. For example, in Westkott's dialectic model (in Messer-Davidow 1985), the researcher compares her findings to her own experience, shares the information with her subjects, and then incorporates their perspectives into the end product. This model is similar to participant feedback, or what Lincoln and Guba (1985) have termed a "member check," in traditional ethnography. Unlike the case of ethnography, however, in feminist research collaboration the expectation is that both the researcher and the participants learn as a result of engaging in the research process: feminist research is a form of consciousness-raising.

Feminist research also acknowledges the subjectivity of the researcher, and the role played by her personal perspective in the construction and interpretation of knowledge (Maher 1983). The researcher is not "an anonymous voice of neutral authority, but a real historical individual with concrete, specific desires and interests" (Harding 1987, 9). This relates to feminism's epistemological notion of intersubjectivity, the view of knowledge as a conglomeration of multiple perspectives. Because feminist researchers never claim or attempt to be detached and impartial, subjectivity is a given, not a weakness, of feminist research.

Acker et al. (1983) pose two questions often asked of feminist researchers by those familiar with traditional methodology; their answers give great insight into the essence of feminist research. To "is the work worthwhile?" they answer that it depends on the original purpose of the research. The purpose of feminist research—to create knowledge that will focus on women's problems and their experience and be beneficial to women—is not the purpose of traditional research. Thus the product of feminist research must be evaluated with a different yardstick: usefulness to the participants. To "is it true?", Acker et al. respond by asking for a clarification of the meaning of truth. In traditional research, truth relates to the ability of the research to predict future occurrences. In feminist research, however, truth is found in an accurate and adequate *reconstruction* of the experience of the researcher and the researched. Thus, feminists have created a body of research with its own conventions and assumptions, one that stands apart from the body of traditional scientific research.[10]

✧ ✧ ✧ ✧ ✧ ✧ ✧

I had anticipated that the opportunity to team-teach with Martha would be the highlight of my fieldwork. She is an exceptional teacher, and her classroom is a special place. During our time together as graduate students we had had the opportunity to collaborate on several different projects and papers. For a variety of reasons our experiences were often less than ideal (in our dialogue journal Martha recalled that ". . . those lovely collaborative curriculum projects . . . were quite trying at times"). But we always enjoyed working together. As Martha said in our dialogue journal; "I tried to think back to the project

---

[10]For a detailed comparison of traditional and feminist research models, please see pages 170–172 in Reinharz's "Experiential analysis: a contribution to feminist research" in Bowles and Klein, eds. *Theories of Women's Studies* (London: Routledge and Kegan Paul, 1983).

with Louise and Nina, and while I often felt on different wavelengths with them about curriculum and planning I felt very comfortable and on the same wavelength with you." So our previous experiences together led us to expect that our collaboration would be a success.

Research also points to the rewards of collaboration. Florio, for example (1978; 1984; 1986), firmly believes in the value of engaging in collaborative research with classroom teachers. She points to the ethical, epistemological, and pragmatic benefits of collaboration: teachers are treated as active subjects rather than objects of study, teacher knowledge is given credence as a legitimate source of information about classroom life, and the findings of collaborative research are likely to have a broader audience, making contributions to both academic and practical knowledge.

Some researchers engaged in collaboration have also alluded to its more problematic aspects. Wilson and her teacher-partners (1993, 89) admit that "although we all agree this work has been exciting, learning to work together has not been easy." Ball and Rundquist (1993, 19) also describe some of the risks and challenges inherent in working together. Collaboration involves wrestling with feelings—your own and those of your partner(s): it is likely to be more complicated than working alone. I knew that some difficulties were bound to arise, and I felt ready to face them.

Martha and I encountered a handful of what I would call "inevitable difficulties" during the course of this study, that is, difficulties which seem to arise in almost every collaborative teaching or research situation. For example, we were both nervous about teaching in front of each other. I worried in my journal:

> Martha says that she is eager to see me in action. I feel a little nervous about teaching in front of her. She is so good, and so different from me. (Field Notes 11/3/94)

> I am a little nervous about preparing materials for use in Martha's classroom. She is so neat, so artistic—her stuff always looks so great. I know that her perception of this is that she is asking the kids to do their best work for her, so she feels that she has to do her best work for them. But I am so haphazard, so messy when it comes to making stuff like this— what will she think? Will she think that I don't care about the kids? (Field Notes 11/13/94)

Martha worried, too.  In our dialogue journal she wrote:

> I must admit before you came, when I was anticipating your coming I was
> in fact quite nervous.  I knew you had high expectations of what my
> teaching and class would be but of course you had never actually seen me
> teach—and I worried that my actual teaching would less than live up to
> your expectations.

We had spent so much time talking about our teaching prior to
the start of this study that each of us worried we wouldn't live up
to the other's high expectations.  Further, I had been out of the
classroom for three years when this study began—would I
remember how to be a teacher?  This worry, too, is not surprising.
Jean Clandinin (1986, 75) experienced similar doubts in her work
on the role of image in teachers' personal practical knowledge.  In
her field notes she wrote:  "On April 30 I took the class alone.  I
felt like a student teacher.  Would I do okay?"

Martha and I also had etiquette problems.  Our first planning
session was a disaster.  We danced around and around, afraid to
step on each other's toes.  Martha described us in our dialogue
journal:  ". . . you saying things to see my response since you are
very aware of the ownership thing—"my" class and classroom.
And I was saying things to see your response to my ideas,
comparing them to yours. . . ."  In my journal, I wrote:

> Martha and I both did a lot of pussyfooting around—neither of us
> wanted to hurt the other's feelings, invade the other's territories (she has
> a class to run, I have a research agenda) . . .  I think that we didn't get
> much accomplished because we were both trying to be too nice to each
> other.
> (Field Notes 11/6/94)

Any collaboration can be difficult.  And when university
researchers enter classrooms, some problems are bound to arise
because of the issues of power and status that are inherent in
these relations.  Though the university researcher may see herself
as little more than the classroom teacher she once was (as I often
did), the view from the classroom is quite different.  For example,
in the work that Professor Deborah Ball and teacher Sylvia
Rundquist did together on issues relating to the teaching of
mathematics, their status differential is immediately visible, even
in print: *Professor* Ball and *teacher* Rundquist.  Though they
called their relationship a collaboration, the two never actually

taught together: "While Deborah teaches, Sylvia watches, and sometimes attends to small tasks in the room" (Ball and Rundquist 1993, 17). Clearly this is not an equal relation.

Rundquist felt she needed help with mathematics instruction, and allowed Ball to teach in her room, hoping that it would enhance her own understanding of math concepts. Though Ball's purpose was not to engage in professional development, Rundquist's confidence as a mathematics teacher blossomed as a result of their work together, and after four years (!) she felt ready to do her own math teaching again. Though their relationship was mutually beneficial, it was not equitable. Ball had more knowledge of mathematics, and Rundquist learned from her. Ball learned too, as a result of her involvement in their relationship, but she did not learn directly from Rundquist.

Other university-based researchers have engaged in work that has been more truly collaborative. Suzanne Wilson, for example, arranged to join a pair of teachers who were already team-teaching. Wilson's duty, to teach social studies four afternoons a week, enabled her to engage in a research project about her own processes of learning to teach. Unlike Ball, Wilson worked closely with her collaborators to plan units and integrate instruction. This was all a part of her research agenda: she admits freely that she never considered what her cooperating teachers might learn from her (Wilson 1993, 89). Part of this is related to her own humility—she had never been an elementary teacher before and consequently did not feel that she had much to offer these experienced professionals—but part of it reflects the self-absorption of university faculty: Wilson had an agenda, and she went into the classroom to get certain things accomplished. The teachers she worked with were happy to have her join them (it gave them an opportunity to leave their classrooms to go to the bathroom during the school day) and the collaboration resulted in learning on both sides of the partnership; but the relationship was never one of equals.

Feminists and other radical researchers have called for the elimination of exploitative research in no uncertain terms. In the field of education, this extends to a refusal to use schools as "data plantations." But is it possible to have a truly collaborative relationship between a researcher and the researched? Or are the two inherently unequal? Only action research—teachers researching their own practices in order to improve their own teaching and enhance their own professional knowledge—comes close to being an oppression-free methodology. As university-based researchers, it seems that the best we can hope for would be a research relationship that approaches a state of symbiosis: research that is mutually beneficial to both the researcher and the researched and hurts no one in the process.

In my research relationship with Martha, I strove for symbiosis, although total symbiosis was simply not possible. We may have planned together and taught together, but, like all university-based researchers, I had my own agenda to attend to as well. Like the overlapping circles of a Venn diagram, there were areas of responsibility that Martha and I shared and areas that we did not. We each had different kinds of power and privilege—Martha could write report cards, hold parent conferences, or refer a child for psychological testing; I could leave the classroom in the middle of the school day, juggle my schedule to meet the needs of my family, or elect to skip school and sit in my office at the university and write instead. But it is also not entirely honest simply to call these responsibilities "different." Though we may have been striving personally for equality within our research relationship, our research was embedded in the larger context of our society. And, for reasons Martha and I could not control, being a teacher lacks the social status of being a university researcher. No matter how we positioned or described the situation, we were not equals.

Even collaborations that are not complicated by these nebulous status issues face inevitable difficulties. Negotiation of territory and stylistic differences are very common challenges of collaborative teaching relationships. And they are often fairly simple to deal with: open communication and flexibility lead directly to workable solutions. But when communication is difficult, collaboration is impaired. Silence and tension hinder partnership and Martha and I learned this lesson the hard way.

The etiquette issues that Martha and I faced as we danced politely around each other during our planning sessions were simply a symptom of larger communication difficulties that posed problems throughout the study. Martha and I may have had a very comfortable and close friendship, but now we had become more than friends (perhaps less than friends?): we were involved in a relationship as researcher and researched, university scholar and classroom practitioner (Florio 1986). Anthropologist

Hortense Powdermaker (1966) suggests that the proper stance of a participant observer is to be both "stranger and friend." But I was not able to be a stranger. I could not bifurcate our relationship that cleanly or completely.

Though we are close friends, our research relationship was tentative and strained. For example, as I mentioned in Chapter Three, I decided that it would be worthwhile for me to lead meeting, hoping that this would help me feel like more of a "real" teacher. When I had originally broached the idea in our dialogue journal, I told Martha that I wanted to lead meeting for the entire month we taught our family unit. But when Martha asked me, face-to-face the next morning, what I wanted to do about leading meeting, I backed down and said that we could play it by ear. In the end, I led meeting only once. And I wondered:

> ...why is it easier to talk to a stranger than a friend?
> (Field Notes 11/1/94)

In her work on relationships in the lives of adolescent girls, Gilligan found that young women's answers to the question, "What is the worst thing that can happen in a relationship?" often dealt with issues of silence and withdrawal: the worst thing that can happen is when one friend starts "building a wall," as one girl said (1990, 22). Though our communication with each other in our personal lives was unaffected, there seemed to be a wall blocking effective communication in our professional relationship.

During the course of the study, Martha and I were able to write about our communication difficulty in our dialogue journal. The dialogue journal was a valuable tool for us: it allowed us to "discuss" uncomfortable issues that would have been too hard to bring up face to face. Martha wrote:

> While I was nervous at first about having you observe, the part I thought that would be the easiest was working together. As it turned out, that was one of the trickier parts. Beyond the horrible planning session where we spent several hours dancing around each other, I was unsure of how involved and what level of time commitment was expected when you were in the different parts of your research. And rather than asking you how much or what you wanted to do I waited for you to ask me. (I figured you are the assertive, "scrutable" one so you'd ask—how was I to know you would worry about impinging on my territory?) I would have been fine having you take the lead and me supporting your teaching.

We did not discuss these problems out loud until we did our final debriefing during the interpretive art activity done when my fieldwork was completed. We spoke as we made clay representations of our teaching. We sat facing each other but were not face to face: we looked down as we talked, busily kneading and shaping our clay. Like nervous teenage girls fidgeting and staring at their shoes as they talk to a popular boy, Martha and I addressed our difficulties:

Martha: .... And I think the other thing is that I would have been very comfortable, and I guess because I have team-taught, with really, like, having you take the lead whenever you wanted to do it.

Lisa: Hmmm ....

Martha: But I felt more awkward asking you to do that because (pause) it's your research, but you (pause) the bottom line is it is my job, and I didn't want you to feel like you were getting saddled with my job when you were trying to do research. So there were things that (pause) I wouldn't have cared if you led meeting the whole time you were here (laughing).

Lisa: I *would* have. But I felt like that would have been barging in too much, that it wouldn't have been appropriate.

Martha: Now, see, I wouldn't have had a problem with it. Um, but I didn't feel like I could ask you to do that either. Because you obviously had different purposes for being here than just teaching. Time to reflect, and all that. Or even the kind of (pause) not just meeting, but things like (pause) I didn't feel it reasonable to ask you to do a lot of prepping and stuff like that because I felt that that wasn't within what you should have had to do.

Lisa: I should have been clearer, then, about what I was willing to do and what I didn't want to do, because I would have been really happy to lead meeting every day the whole time I was here, I would have been really happy to do all the prep work, because that is part of being a teacher, that's a real part of it.

Martha: But I think you, too, had a lot of, from what we talked about, issues of territory and things like that, which doesn't even phase me at all. Maybe it's because I have team-taught before. And I am used to sharing a space. And in many situations it would have been much easier to team-teach with you than with some of the people that I had to team-teach with! And I also don't feel (pause) threatened by somebody else (pause), I don't feel as territorial about it, in a way, and so I don't feel like it is threatening to have somebody else move into my world. I don't know.

Martha knew that we had different reasons for coming to Room 4 each morning. There were different kinds of work to be done, and someone had to do each kind. Martha said that she did not feel comfortable asking me to do certain tasks, like prep work or leading meeting because, as she said, "the bottom line is it is my job, and I didn't want you to feel like you were getting saddled with my job when you were trying to do research." She knew that I "obviously had different purposes for being here than just teaching. Time to reflect, and all that," and said, "I didn't feel it reasonable to ask you to do a lot of prepping and stuff like that because I felt that that wasn't within what you should have had to do."

I, on the other hand, was eager to participate in the fullness of being a teacher. No job was too mundane. But I felt uncomfortable about asserting myself when I was a guest in someone else's territory: "I felt like that would have been barging in too much, that it wouldn't have been appropriate." Martha's view of our particular job responsibilities and professional agendas kept her from asking for my help, and my worries about territory and boundaries kept me from offering. One simple and straightforward conversation was all we would have needed to straighten out this silly misunderstanding.

And why *hadn't* we been able to have a straightforward conversation about this situation while my fieldwork was in progress? Any attempts we made to deal with these issues only clouded them further and heightened the tensions around them. Jean Clandinin's (1993) notion of "storying" sheds some light on our frustrating and counterproductive situation. Clandinin maintains that our lives are "storied": as people we are shaped by our race, class, gender, culture, ethnicity, institutions, and professions, and by the ways that these factors interact with our unique experiences in the world. We can make sense of what we do "both as living our stories in an ongoing experiential text and as telling our stories in word as we reflect on life and explain ourselves to others" (1993, 1). We are "constantly telling and re-telling stories . . . that both refigure the past and create purpose in the future" (Connelly and Clandinin 1990, 4).

In addition to storying and restorying ourselves, we also story those around us. We hear their stories, and then we create our own story about them. Sometimes our story includes their story, sometimes it does not. An example might help make this point more clear. Pat Hogan, the director of a teacher training program in Canada, was faced with the problem of dealing with an unhappy and unsuccessful student teacher, Joanne. She and the cooperating teacher, Carol, were trying to make sense of Joanne's trouble. Hogan writes:

> I, too, began to try to construct a story around what was happening. I was puzzled over the differences between the way Carol told the story of the relationship and what I sensed was happening for Joanne . . . . I started to think of Joanne as being overwhelmed and unable to fulfill the expectations set up for her. The story I was constructing seemed to be validated when I learned more about Carol's vision of team-teaching and her expectations for Joanne as a member of that team. Perhaps I needed a story that would reduce my frustration with Joanne's silence and allow me to see some future for her. By this time Carol's frustration had led her to consult with the principal regarding Joanne's apparent lack of progress. The principal had a talk with Joanne and storied the possibility of her failure in the practicum . (1993, 111)

When Joanne finally was given a chance to tell her story, it did not match the ones that her cooperating teacher and supervisors in the program had constructed for her. All the conflicting and competing stories obscured the true nature of the situation.

Some of the communication difficulties that Martha and I experienced stemmed, I believe, from the stories I myself created. I have storied myself as a headstrong and forceful person (I referred to myself in our dialogue journal as "a real steamroller when I'm not careful"). In my life as a teacher I am usually very certain about what I believe is right, and am not hesitant to act. I have always been very territorial, feeling a strong sense of ownership of my classroom. But I had storied this research project to be as equal a partnership as possible. As a result, I had to be very careful. I respected Martha's classroom practices and tried to fit into her manner of teaching, even when it went against my gut teacherly instincts. I tried to avoid stepping on Martha's toes, infringing on her territory, cramping her style.

I also storied Martha. I storied her to be as territorial as I am, projecting my own feelings onto her. As a result of my storying of the situation, no matter how many times she encouraged me to take charge and to play any role in classroom life that I wanted to play, I was hesitant to do so. For example, I wrote:

> Martha says that I am welcome to take the reins at any time, but it doesn't feel like she means it.
> (Field Notes 11/6/94)

> Although Martha said that she felt okay about me doing meeting, I never got the sense that I was welcome to do it. I don't know why.
> (Field Notes 11/20/94)

Now I know why. Clandinin's notion of storying suggests that the mysterious sense of discomfort I felt relates directly to the ways that I storied myself and Martha. I had storied Martha in a way that prevented me from hearing the things she was saying to me, and from hearing her own story of herself as a teacher.

I must also consider the impact of Martha's own stories about herself, and about me, on our communication difficulties. She storied herself as open, willing, and relaxed about collaborating in the classroom, as the conversation I cited earlier illustrates ("I would have been very comfortable, and I guess because I have team-taught, with really, like, having you take the lead whenever you wanted to do it"). She did indeed tell me on many different occasions that I was welcome to take over at any time; but somehow I remained unconvinced. In my previous interpretation of the situation, I had blamed myself, but could I also point the finger at Martha? Was I unconvinced because on some level, Martha was actually sending out mixed messages? I do not know how Martha storied me, but I am confident that it influenced the unfolding of our collaboration.

As a result of my storying of the situation, I felt tentative as a guest in Martha's classroom. In my journal I wrote:

> I don't want to intrude, or push too far . . .
> (Field Notes 11/6/94)

I feared that pushing too far or too hard would put a strain on our professional relationship, and was also worried about repercussions our work might have in our personal relationship. I did not want to jeopardize our life as friends. Like the women in Carol Gilligan's (1982) landmark study of ethical decision making, I often acted out of a desire to preserve our interpersonal connection. Gilligan describes the world of the women she interviewed as "a world of relationships and psychological truths where an awareness of the connection between people gives rise to a recognition of responsibility for one another, a perception of the need for response" (1982, 30). She depicts a web of relationship that needs to be sustained.

In thinking about the difficulties I encountered while collaborating with Martha, I reflected on my own behavior and responses. I noticed that decisions I had made seemed out of character—I referred to myself in my journal as "wimpy," and "passive." Reflecting on some activities that did not go as well as we had hoped, I wrote:

> And I think that some of the stuff we did—the genetics discussion, perhaps, and the songs for certain—would have benefitted from my being the teacher to introduce them. I guess I should have asserted myself more. Gee, it's hard to believe that I would ever write THOSE words! (Field Notes 11/20/94)

Not being assertive enough was a problem I had never dreamed I would encounter. I was mystified by my own behavior.

Further, I was aware that this unusual turn of events might be damaging to my dissertation findings. As I wrote in my journal:

> Is it possible that I won't be able to do any real research on my curriculum planning and decision making either, because of the dicey nature of the co-teaching relationship? Did I fuck myself again????? (Field Notes 11/6/94)

The profanity and the desperate, imploring punctuation suggest that I was deeply concerned about how our relationship was affecting my data collection. But I did not change my behavior. I was not able to act in any other way, as if I needed to protect and sustain our friendship at any cost. In addition to the challenge of the research, I had also taken on the responsibility for doing the maintenance work necessary to sustain and preserve our intimacy, our personal relationship.

A concrete example of my efforts to protect our relationship comes from one of our conversational interviews. I spoke with Martha about deliberate activities she engages in with the students in order to build a sense of community in the classroom. She responded by discussing a conflict resolution program that she had started to do with her class in the afternoons. I was surprised, because nine of the twenty-four children in the class were kindergartners who go home for the day just before lunch:

> Lisa: So you're doing things that build a sense of community without having the whole community present, in that case.
>
> Martha: Uh-huh. Well, I still do the conflict resolution stuff, I would still do it with the youngers, but not as a group.
>
> Lisa: They also will get it, I think (pause), they'll absorb it from living in that kind of environment.

Rather than push the point that Martha's community-building activities were taking place with more than a third of the community not present, I backpedaled, agreeing with her when I had intended to disagree. I did not get that triumphant feeling "gotcha!" that often accompanies the discovery of a significant discrepancy: I quickly invented a solution that would help her decision make sense to me, willing to let my principles slip in order to sustain our relationship, in order to preserve our sense of consensus regarding educational values.

Glossing over this inconsistency also allowed me to keep my story of Martha intact. I had storied her as an exemplary teacher, above reproach. Now she had admitted doing community-building activities with only a fraction of her class present, a practice I thought foolish, if not counterproductive, and which contradicted my story. But I found it easier to backpedal than to restory the situation. My relationship with Martha means a great deal to me, and I hold her in high regard, so I could not allow her to be less than perfect. I found it easier to cling tenaciously to my story than to allow Martha to tell me *her* story.

Martha and I both engaged in this maintenance work. In a dialogue journal discussion of our difficult planning session, Martha made excuses for us:

> I tried to think back to the project [that we did as graduate students] with
> Louise and Nina, and while I often felt on different wavelengths with
> them about curriculum and planning I felt very comfortable and on the
> same wavelength with you. On Saturday I didn't feel on any wavelength
> at all. Am I just burnt out from all the stress of planning, teaching,
> conferencing, and parent flack?

It was easier to blame burnout than to suggest that we were
having a relational problem. Later in the same entry, after writing
with a fair degree of bluntness about our difficult planning
session, Martha wrote; "I'm not at all sure what I have been
rambling on about. This purple pen must have a mind of its
own." It was too difficult and dangerous for Martha to own the
honest thoughts about our difficulties. Martha's evil purple pen
said those terrible things—just as my toddler's stuffed monkey
has a tendency to misbehave and hit the baby.

The desire to preserve and protect my relationship with
Martha is a strong one. In fact, it has made the writing of this
chapter very difficult. Making our difficulties public feels like a
dangerous risk to our connection.[11] When I designed this study, I
think I expected the relational chapter to be about the ways in
which our friendship made our team-teaching easier, more
rewarding, more connected, more feminist. But when the research
got underway and things did not go in that direction, I started
having second thoughts about this chapter, and tried to downplay
the value of looking at our relationship. At several points during
my fieldwork I even decided to eliminate the chapter altogether. I
wrote in my journal:

> I think that the relational strand might turn into a small methodological
> appendix as [one of my reviewers] suggested. Though I think it's
> somewhat important to my work, my relationship with Martha is not
> yielding data.... I do think that it is important to mention and to explore
> to a certain degree, but I don't think that it should be a focus. I don't
> think that it sheds much light on love-based teaching, either.
> (Field Notes 10/22/94)

Does it even make sense to have a relational strand at all? Hmmm . . . I

---

[11]See Ball and Rundquist (1993) for a similar problem. Writing the story of their
collaboration exposed Rundquist's lack of mathematical knowledge and
confidence, and put her at risk for embarrassment and humiliation. Making their
story public felt like a professional risk for Rundquist.

don't think that I will be able to write a whole chapter about the role of love in our teaching relationship. The stuff was strictly interpersonal . . . (Field Notes 12/5/94)

Though it was not deliberate, it seems that I was willing to alter my carefully developed plans, and dismiss my research agenda, to protect our relationship.

One of the purposes of the relational study had been to explore the ways that love and our shared commitment to teaching with love affected our teaching collaboration. As Sternberg describes it, love comprises the interplay of intimacy, commitment, and passion: thus far I have focused on the first component, intimacy. Martha and I entered this study with high levels of intimacy, and our feelings of closeness and friendship and our desire to sustain our personal relationship had an enormous influence on our co-teaching experience. As this chapter has illustrated, our level of intimacy was both a help and a hindrance to our work, and was certainly the most significant force in shaping our collaboration.

In the case of our co-teaching relationship, passion and commitment refer not to our feelings about one another but to our feelings about teaching. Martha and I shared a strong commitment to our co-teaching relationship. We did our best to navigate the interpersonal challenges involved, never doubting that, with time and effort, our team-teaching would be a success. We based this conclusion, I believe, on our shared passion for teaching. Teaching, and teaching well, matters deeply to us both. When our communication difficulties fogged us in, as occurred in the particularly disastrous planning session that I mentioned earlier in this chapter, our passion for teaching was a beacon that helped us find our way.

When Sternberg's triangular theory of love is displayed in graphic form (as it was in Chapter One), the triangle represented is usually equilateral (see Figure 2). Love is thus depicted as involving *equal amounts* of passion, intimacy, and commitment. But this representation is misleading, and obscures the flexibility inherent in Sternberg's model. Sternberg asserts that all three components need to be present in order for consummate love to exist. However, they do not need to be present in equal amounts. A loving relationship can be characterized as having a great deal of commitment and intimacy but little passion, a great deal of passion and intimacy but little commitment, and so on.

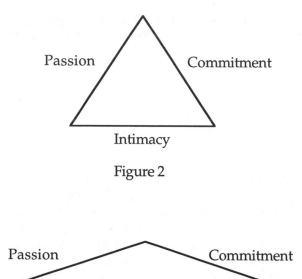

Figure 2

Figure 3

In the case of Martha's and my co-teaching relationship, love took this shape (see Figure 3). Issues of intimacy loomed very large in shaping our co-teaching experience, but were balanced by our commitment to the act of collaborating and to our shared passion for teaching. In fact, it is commitment and passion that pulled us through the difficult challenges we faced in collaborating.

Our lopsided triangle suggests that Glesne and Peshkin (1992), cited earlier in this chapter, may have been right: don't do a backyard study. In the case of Martha's and my collaboration, intimacy was the starting point, and I believe this was the root of our difficulties; basing a research or team-teaching relationship on passion for the act of teaching and commitment to the collaborative process might have been more fruitful and less challenging. In that case, intimacy would have developed naturally as a byproduct of the lived experience of collaboration.

Moving beyond issues of love, my experience with Martha raises many other kinds of questions that have ramifications for teachers and researchers engaged in collaboration. If, as Gilligan's

(1982) work suggests, many women share the tendency to focus on preserving and maintaining relationships, women-dominated fields such as teaching are likely to be colored by this perspective on decision making. What is gained by giving primacy to relationships in collaborative teaching and research endeavors? And what is the cost? Do we seem less professional when we focus on preserving relationships? Do teachers and researchers with this orientation seem "cloying and cozy" (Acker In press), instead of intellectual? Does a commitment to sustaining interpersonal connection, what I have labelled "maintenance work," hinder professional growth and development? Is our research tainted somehow by this tendency? Are all research collaborations doomed to dance some variation on the dance that characterized my experience with Martha?

Feminist ethics and research methodologies suggest that focusing on relationships is an asset, not a liability. If this way of looking at the world seems less professional, less scientific, the problem may be with the terms "scientific" and "professional," not with the perspective of care. Scientific and professional are limited terms, terms that are not always relevant. The perspective they represent is far too narrow to include many of the most important facets of any human encounter, including educational research.

And I do believe that all collaborative relationships are destined to be dances, though "doomed" may be a harsh way of describing this inevitable state of affairs. All collaborative work involves ongoing renegotiation and constant give-and-take. The dance is an inevitable part of the process, and it is not a problem unless the dancers perceive it as one.

And what about storying? The act of storying seems inextricably linked with the act of making meaning, an inevitable part of life in a constructivist, postmodern world. Teachers and researchers alike story the people with whom they work. But we must remain vigilant against letting our own stories obscure the possibility of alternative explanations of situations and experiences. Storying itself is not problematic, but it becomes dangerous, as it was for me in my work with Martha, when its influence on thinking and perception goes unnoticed.

# 6
## Issues in Teaching with Love

Looking closely at Martha's teaching and my own has allowed me to develop a preliminary understanding of the nature of love in early childhood classrooms, and to identify a particular constellation of feelings which I have labelled "teacherly love." It is true that some researchers have suggested that it is not possible or desirable for teachers to love their students (Freud 1952; Lightfoot 1977). Jules Henry (1963, 30) asserts that even those teachers who claim to love their students do not but are really just exaggerating their affectionate feelings: "If that were not so, children would have to be dragged shrieking from grade to grade and most teachers would flee teaching, for the mutual attachment would be so deep that its annual severing would be too much for either to bear."

Even Mem Fox, one of the writers whose name I have invoked to support my case for teaching with love, takes issue with the notion of teachers loving the children entrusted to them. She writes:

> Let me tighten my definition of love and passion, lest I be misunderstood. I am not asking the unreasonable from literacy teachers. I am not, for instance, asking that all the children in a class should be loved since love cannot be mandated and anyway not all children are lovable. I am asking rather for a loving atmosphere in which students and their interests are treated with dignity; an environment in which they are seen as exciting, fascinating beings who are alive with anticipation and longing for real communication that has great meaning in their current lives, not in some far-distant adult life; a system in which they never sit in corridors and suffer lovelessness; a classroom from which worksheets and basal readers have been withdrawn and burnt with ritual and ceremony in the schoolyard; in which there is a throbbing heartbeat of passion connecting the class to itself and the teacher to the class. (1995, 13)

Mem Fox eschews actual love for students in favor of the creation of "a loving atmosphere," throbbing with the heartbeat of passion. But how significant is this distinction?

Progressive educator Herb Kohl also eschews love for students, in his case in favor of the notion of "loving students as learners." He writes:

> It is important to pause over the idea of *loving students as learners*, which is not the same as simply loving students. Each of us has only a limited amount of love we can offer, for love is not cheaply won or given. I care about all of my students, and respect them, but love grows slowly and requires attention and effort that cannot be spread around to twenty or thirty people simultaneously. Love also engages all parts of one's life, and teaching, for all its demands, is still just a part of one's total life as a parent, lover, citizen, and learner. I don't trust teachers who say they love all their students, because it isn't possible to love so many people you know so little about and will separate from in six months or a year. (1984, 64)

Both Fox and Kohl, though quite interested in love, reject the idea of teachers genuinely loving their students. I believe this is because they share an implicit assumption at the root of their distinctions between "love" and engaging with students in some other kind of loving way that is more appropriate for classroom life. When Kohl and Fox use the word "love" and refer to it as something that is not acceptable for describing relations or interactions between teachers and students, they are assuming that there is only one monolithic, general kind of love. They list some of its characteristics. It is a love that cannot be mandated, a love that is not cheaply won or given. It grows slowly and requires attention and effort. It cannot be spread around to a large group of individuals at the same time. It engages all parts of one's life. Not all children call it forth. It cannot start and stop arbitrarily.

Mem Fox and Herb Kohl both seem to believe that there is only one type of love, namely an emotion or feeling that would be appropriate to apply to relationships with family and close friends, but not with students. They are making the same error that I made when I thought that I did not love Martha's students: they are conflating a variety of possible types of love. As I discovered during the course of my self-study and described in Chapter Three, there exists a distinct state of mind or set of feelings which can be called "teacherly love." It is a unique kind of love, and only one of a number of possible varieties of love—eros, agape, motherly love, brotherly love, spousal love, love for friends, and so on. A teacher may certainly feel love for her students, but it will be a kind of love different from the love she feels for her spouse, children, parents, or friends. Teacherly love is like other kinds of love in some ways, but it is also unlike other forms of love.

Kohl's idea of loving students as learners is teacherly love by another name. Mem Fox's depiction of a loving classroom environment is one suffused with teacherly love. In their descriptions of the ways that love is not appropriate for teachers and students, both Fox and Kohl have actually given us their own definitions of teacherly love. The teachers to whom Jules Henry referred in the passage I quoted earlier (depicting the children shrieking in anguish at the end of the school year) are not exaggerating their feelings as he suggests. Those teachers actually do feel love for their students: they feel teacherly love. Much of the literature on teaching in which teachers, both real and fictional, tell their own stories, are tales of teacherly love: *Teacher* (Ashton-Warner 1963), *Up the Down Staircase* (Kaufman 1964), *Being With Children* (Lopate 1975), *36 Children* (Kohl 1967), *Among Schoolchildren* (Kidder 1989), sections of Bill Ayers' *To Teach* (1993), some of the stories retold in Schubert and Ayers's *Teacher Lore* (1992), and *To Sir, with Love* (Braithwaite 1959). The research on elementary schools as workplaces and on elementary schoolteachers' job satisfaction (Acker In press; Nias 1989; Hargreaves 1994) is also rich with narratives of teacherly love.

This plenitude suggests that teacherly love is no more monolithic than other forms of love. Like Mem Fox and Herb Kohl, every teacher is likely to have his or her own definition, emphasizing the aspects of working and living life in relation to students that are most pertinent for his or her teaching practices. In this study I specifically explored ways in which teacherly love played out in the classroom lives of two teachers who both claim to root their teaching practices in love. Nevertheless, I do think some generalizations can be made, and that the concept of teacherly love does have broad applicability: one does not need to be a loving teacher or to be teaching with practices self-consciously rooted in love to feel teacherly love for one's students. In this chapter I will be focusing on the parameters of teacherly love as it occurs specifically within the broader notion of deliberately loving teaching.

First, teacherly love is similar to other, better documented forms of love. As I discussed in Chapter Four, teacherly love is similar to motherly love. It is more limited in scope, duration, and intensity than the love that a mother feels for her children, but teacherly love and motherly love share much common ground. It is also like agape, the Christian concept of neighbor-love (Outka 1972) in its focus on giving affection to others for their own sakes. Unlike agape, however, teacherly love is not deliberately selfless: most teachers who love their students expect to receive something in return, be it love from the students or some kind of inherent job satisfaction.     Further, teacherly love does not depend on inspiration from God as agape does.

Teacherly love is also distinct from other forms of love. An examination of the loving teaching practices depicted in this study provides insight into the unique nature of teacherly love.     First, teacherly love is rooted in commitment.     Teacherly love arises when a belief in the value of love in education and a deliberate decision to love students combine with a passion for teaching; and it grows as a result of the intimacy that occurs in the life of a loving classroom.     Unlike other forms of love, then, teacherly love can be bidden.     My experience as co-teacher in Martha's classroom and as teacher of record in my own classroom illustrate this.     I entered Martha's classroom with nothing more than the commitment to enter into loving relationships with her students, and though it took time, those relationships did develop.     As my teaching journal entries also illustrate, teacherly love can begin as merely the commitment to love, and then become transformed into something fuller and richer with the passing of time and the development of intimacy.

If teacherly love is a commitment, a professional responsibility, then by extension all students must be considered worthy of teacherly love.     If a teacher elects to let love play a role in her teaching practices, then she must be prepared to try to find something to love in each child.     Just as she has a responsibility to try to teach each child to read and to calculate, she also has a responsibility to try to feel teacherly love for each child.

Teacherly love can be bidden but, like all other forms of love, it cannot be forced.     Even a strong commitment to love may not be enough to cause genuine teacherly loving feelings to develop.     My difficulties loving Gus bear this out.     Further, teacherly love may be unrequited: it is possible to imagine a teacher loving students who do not want to be loved, or who resist entering into any kind of relationship with the teacher.     A loving teacher needs to accept these responses. Understanding and making sense of gaps in love is a difficult and problematic aspect of teacherly love, a crease in its fabric that cannot be smoothed away.

Second, teacherly love is rooted in experience. Feminist philosophers (Noddings 1984; Ruddick 1989; Held 1987) see the ethic of care growing out of the experience of mothering, and the ways in which engaging in the caring labor of mothering contributes to this perspective on morality and decision making. Similarly, engaging in the act of teaching with love leads to the development of teacherly love, which is thus rooted in the experience of loving teaching. For both Martha and me, it was through our lived experiences as classroom teachers that we arrived at our commitment to teach with love as a guiding force in our practice. Further, teacherly love is a form of personal practical knowledge (Clandinin 1986), a way of knowing that is connected to our everyday lives as teachers of young children. As a result, being loving is more than just one of the personality traits of a loving teacher: teaching with love is an intellectual act, a manifestation of a particular kind of knowledge.

Third, teacherly love is distinctly different from other forms of love, in several significant ways. First, teacherly love almost always begins as a commitment to love, a commitment which is fulfilled as intimacy develops over the natural course of classroom life. Unlike most other forms of love, teacherly love can often begin quite quickly: my teaching journal dates the start of loving feelings for my second graders as September 24, not even three weeks into the school year. Teacherly love also has a highly unusual shape. Most loving relationships involve simple pairs of individuals, with an occasional and complicated three-person "love triangle." Teacherly love, on the other hand, could be considered a "love polygon," a loving relationship involving one teacher and a group of children.

But the most significant difference between teacherly love and all other forms of love is that teacherly love is shaped and constrained by the academic calendar and the structures of the institution of schooling. To borrow a phrase from the arena of romantic love, teacherly love relationships are always September-to-June affairs. Like fools for love, teachers enter into relationships knowing full well they will not last. Each year, the cycle of teacherly love plays itself out in classrooms. Children arrive, relationships grow and blossom. In June, the gorgeous blossoms are picked while in full bloom. The end of the school year is a difficult time for loving teachers, as both Jules Henry (1963) and my own teaching journal suggest: "If I had only liked Alesha instead of allowing myself to love her, I would not feel so sad" (Teaching Journal 6/6/91). There may be no shrieking children or fleeing teachers, but the annual severing of mutual attachment is painful nonetheless. And then the summer, when, like aging cut flowers drooping in a vase, teacherly love wilts, its petals drop slowly, and its colors fade. The cycle is ready to begin again with the start of the new school year.

Though it is possible to draw some general conclusions about the nature and characteristics of love's role in education, there is much that cannot be generalized. Teaching with love, like all other kinds of loving relationships, is an essentially human phenomenon. It is highly specific, and cannot be reduced to a list of factors or components without being eviscerated. Chapter Two was a study of Martha's teaching practices, and Chapter Three a study of my own; together they demonstrate how loving teaching takes very different shapes when molded by the hands and minds of different teachers. Like love, loving teaching is not a monolithic entity. Because love is so deeply personal, so rooted in lived experience and personal style, it is possible to imagine that there are as many varieties of loving teaching as there are loving teachers. This is one of the problematic, complicated aspects of teaching with love.

A close examination of the role of love in my teaching and in Martha's bears this out. In many ways, the forms of loving teaching that Martha and I practice are diametrically opposed. For example, Martha values and emphasizes process and experience. She said in our dialogue journal: "Content knowledge or fact knowledge is somewhat secondary to me than process knowledge and/or the experience of just trying things out." I, too, value process and experience, but I also feel a strong sense of responsibility to the content being taught. I worried that Martha's laissez-faire attitude about the presentation of activities caused some of the students in our class to lack clarity of purpose: they did not always know why they were doing what they were doing, and while that was fine with Martha, it troubled me. I was similarly concerned about Martha's relaxed approach to assessment.

Another set of polar opposites in our visions of teaching with love are our units of analysis, the essential organizing element of our teaching. In Martha's teaching the unit of analysis is the individual; in my teaching the unit of analysis is the group. Martha's classroom experience is centered on the children as individuals. Each child has the opportunity to craft his or her own educational menu each day, selecting from the offerings that Martha makes available. Organizing her classroom with activity stations rather than whole group instruction allows Martha maximum flexibility in meeting the individual needs of each child. When Martha takes an active role in placing children at activity stations, she makes her decisions by carefully considering the needs, interests, and capabilities of each child as an individual. Martha made this aspect of her practice explicit in our dialogue journal. She wrote: "It is very important to me that I respond to each child as an individual, which means really knowing them."

By contrast, in my teaching practices, as reflected both in my experience in Martha's classroom and in the journal entries from my last year as a self-contained classroom teacher, I focus less on the individual children and more on the class as a group, or as I called it then, "a family of learners." I elaborated on this further: "Although I do love the individual children and cherish their personalities and gifts, what I *really* get off on, what really sends me, is the process of taking a bunch of individuals and turning them (us) into a cohesive group, a community with a culture all its own." My approach to classroom discipline reflects this orientation. When witnessing a serious disagreement between students, such as Gus and Rita's mathematics showdown, or Peter and Mark's difficulties sharing a book, my response is to step in and help defuse the situation, thus enabling the children to fulfill their responsibility to maintain the cohesion of the group.

This example highlights a third significant difference in our versions of teaching with love: teacher presence. Martha chooses to be an implicit presence in her classroom. She hangs back, lets the children solve their own problems, waits for community to develop organically, and allows the students to determine the success or failure of any particular activity. As an illustration of her image of the classroom as child-centered and child-led, Martha said, "I never have the upper hand. Always remember that!" Of course, the classroom would not function as smoothly as it does were it not for the structure that Martha has carefully built.  She simply prefers to downplay her importance, her centrality.

My tendency to rush in to help students solve problems illustrates my desire to have an explicit presence in the classroom settings in which I work.  From my desire to open our co-taught family unit with hoopla and ceremony to the deliberate and concerted efforts I made in my own classroom to develop a sense of community, I put myself into the center of the action.  I take a great deal of joy in participating directly in the life of my classroom, and never hesitate to get involved.

This contrast between Martha's classroom presence and my own points to the role played by personality in teaching with love.  Though this is an oversimplification, suffice it to say that Martha is reserved, "inscrutable" even, while I am effusive, or, as Martha wrote in our dialogue journal, eminently "scrutable."  This fundamental difference in our personalities leads to fundamental differences in our teaching styles and in our visions of loving teaching.

For example, our approaches to self-revelation in the classroom reflect our different personalities.  I look for opportunities to share myself with my students.  When they are doing writing activities, such as the "House Is a House for Me" books I mentioned in Chapter Two, I will often join them, writing my own story.  I see a need to model the kind of openness and willingness to take risks that I would like to see in my students.  And my self-revelations lead to greater intimacy and a strengthening of our community.  The more we know about each other, the closer we will feel:  I see self-revelation as a tool for building relationships.  Martha's approach is just the opposite.  She will not reveal herself to anyone until she feels that a relationship has been established:  "I don't do that with people I don't have an established caring relationship with.  I just don't.  It's not me.  Part of me knows that I've reached that level when I'm ready to start sharing."

Personality and personal style influence all teachers' work.  It has been said about teachers that we do not teach what we know, we teach who we are.  Jean Clandinin's work on imagery in teaching (1986) suggests that in addition to these personal factors, teachers' practices are guided and shaped by central images or metaphors.  For example, the central image of my teaching is a metaphor of the "family of learners."  As I have pointed out, I made a conscious effort to create this type of atmosphere in my classroom. Perhaps I even saw myself as the matriarch of the family, hence my willingness to be directive (or perhaps even manipulative) at times.

The central image of Martha's teaching, I believe, is embodied in her dialogue journal statement, "It is very important to me that I respond to each child as an individual which means really knowing them, which means investing in them emotionally." Martha's commitment to "really knowing them" as individuals is the organizing force in her loving teaching: her classroom is organized in a way that allows for her to come to know and respond to each child as an individual with unique needs, expectations, and desires. Martha and I have contrasting images of our practice, and as a result, engage in very different forms of loving teaching. Our contrasting images were one of the reasons it was difficult for me to feel like a "real" teacher while in Martha's classroom: I had to check my central image at the door, so to speak.

As our personalities, central images, and teaching styles differ, so do our versions of teaching with love. We do share a commitment to letting love play a role in our teaching practices, but loving teaching, like all teaching, is shaped by each teacher's personality and by her image of classroom life. This observation raises important and difficult questions. Does the shared commitment to love which undergirds our teaching make Martha and me more like each other than like teachers who do not teach with love as a guiding force? Should I abandon the term "teacherly love" and replace it with "teacherly loves," a term which would better capture the multiplicity, the range of possibilities, inherent in teaching with love? This term implies that the similarities between us are more significant, more powerful, than the differences.

But that might not be the case: our fundamental differences might overshadow our philosophical common ground. For example, in addition to being a loving teacher, Martha is an exemplary early childhood educator, implementing developmentally appropriate practices in her classroom to a remarkably high and consistent degree. Is Martha more similar to another exemplary early childhood educator who does not think that love should play a role in her teaching, or to a university professor of mathematics who is an advocate of the value of passion, commitment, and intimacy in her teaching? Love is a word, like democracy, or freedom, or inquiry, that means different things to different people. Within the context of this narrow study I was not able to determine whether the similarities or the differences in our loving teaching practices were more important.

One surprising finding of this research was the degree to which love can be a difficult and problematic term in the context of the education of young children. In exploring the nature of love in classroom life as described in this book, I experienced and considered a phenomenon that I have labelled "teacherly love." But I did not invent the notion of teacherly love: teacherly love has existed for as long as there have been teachers and students. It is a real part of life for many teachers, but a"feeling that has no name" (Friedan 1963). It is widely experienced, informally acknowledged, but rarely discussed. In this study I merely name the feeling and bring teacherly love out into the open.

But it seems that some teachers who feel teacherly love, like Herb Kohl and Mem Fox, reject the word "love." Even Martha, who agreed to participate in this study on love in classrooms because of the important role that love plays in her teaching practices, is ambivalent about the utility of the word "love" in the context of elementary teaching. Martha admits freely that her relationships with the children drive her practice:

> I need that connection to them . . . It is an interaction that goes back and forth. . . . They know how I feel about them, and they in turn can give that to me. And then, because they give it to me, I can give it back to them. I think that it influences my level of excitement at being with them. It influences me in terms of I want to pick things that they'll love because I want them to love whatever is going on in my class. I think it makes me very thoughtful about things. . . . It's not enough for me to know that Mark is negative. I want to know why, how I can influence that, how I can manage the environment to downplay it for him.

When Martha represented her teaching in clay, she rolled out four long strands and braided them together. Then she twisted the braid around on itself, connecting the two ends to create a gnarled and tangled circle. When I asked her to give it a name she proffered "Metamorphosis," and described it like this:

> It changes and transforms, but it's all connected. It morphs into different shapes. And I feel that is really true in here [the classroom]. It always changes. And I almost feel like anything I've said about it at one moment

would be different in the next moment. It is really hard to capture it. It's really evolving and changing, and then it's all very interwoven, too.

When I asked her to label the four strands, she replied: "The children. Me. The environment. And my philosophy." It is not surprising that Martha started her list with the children. They are the center of the universe she has created in Room 4, and all that occurs in the classroom is in direct response to the children and their needs. Intimacy, in the form of Martha's relationships with the children, is the most important part of her teaching experience. Early in her career Martha worked as a substitute teacher in the Boston area and was very unhappy. She hated showing alcohol abuse films in high school one day and passing out worksheets in third grade the next. A substitute might be doing the same job as a teacher, but it was not the same experience, she said. Martha realized that, for her, "what was really important about [teaching] was having a relationship with the children, and having the continuity of that."

Despite all these powerful relational feelings, Martha is hesitant to use the word "love" to describe her relationships with the students. In our dialogue journal she wrote:

> It feels strange even to use the word love in writing or talking about students not because I don't feel love, but because I generally don't think it is expected and in some people's eyes acceptable and/or good to love students. So while I feel it, I would not often speak about my relationships with students in those terms.

Martha feels love for her students, but is resistant to using the word "love." She feels love, yet "would not often speak about [her] relationships with students in those terms." Why? Is this a simple issue of semantics? Or is there something so problematic about the word "love" that it cannot be uttered in educational contexts?

In a later conversation I asked Martha if she specifically intended to create a love-filled classroom, and she continued her ambivalence: "Um, I don't know, cause that word still seems so much more slippery to me. Like, I, in day care I would have said yes in a minute. But it still seems weird for me to say that, that that's my intention, in an elementary school."

It seems that Martha does love the children, but doesn't love "love." It is a loaded word, "slippery," as Martha said. It means

different things to different people.  Parents might not feel
comfortable with the idea of a teacher loving their children.

Just prior to beginning my fieldwork, I wrote a letter to the
parents of Martha's students, introducing myself and explaining a
bit about my research.  Both Martha and Alexander, her principal,
specifically requested that I not use the word "love" in my letter
to the parents.  It was okay for me to talk about caring and
relationships, but not love.  The Bayview parent community could
be difficult at times, they said, and they did not want to create
any more trouble than was brewing already.  Again, the word
"love" was dismissed.  Martha and Alexander positioned their
request as a public relations issue.  But the silence around love
suggests that the issue is larger than that.

How did teacherly love come to be the feeling that has no
name?  Since it is widely acknowledged to exist, why has it not
been researched?  Why has this particular facet of teaching gone
undiscussed and unrecognized in academe?

Throughout this book I have suggested some possible reasons
for this ambivalence about love and about love's role in classroom
life.  In Chapter One I point to evidence from the history of the
discipline of early childhood education.  The early practitioners in
this nascent field were eager for their work to appear scientific
and professional, thereby gaining recognition and higher status for
it.  Thus science was adopted, and caring discarded.

The issue of appropriate professional image and behavior
arises again in the context of Martha's teaching, in Chapter Four.
She believes that the parents of her students might shy away from
love because "some see letting emotions get involved as
unprofessional."  The literature on the relationship between
teachers and mothers cited in that chapter (Katz 1981; Lightfoot
1977, 1978; Biklen 1992) also points this out.  Mothering and
teaching are thought to have clearly different scopes and
purviews; teaching with love stands in the murky gray area
between the two.

Martha also suggests that the parents' "own experience with
school and teachers might dictate a lot of their thinking about
what schooling should be."  In other words, parents are
envisioning their children's educations by looking backward, at
their own past experiences.  Loving teaching's potential for
contributing to the education of young children, then, is tightly
constrained by the stranglehold of the past: society's vision of

what is possible in schooling is controlled by memories of the way things have always been done. One of the implicit purposes of this study is to make public the beneficial contributions of love to education, and to acknowledge the contributions that love has been making to education all along.

However, I do not wish to suggest that love is a completely unproblematic set of feelings when applied to education. As I mentioned in Chapter Three, Alice Miller's (1983) work on poisonous pedagogy reminds us that very unloving things can be done to children in the name of love. "Love" is a term that can be twisted and stretched to cover an inordinately large area of behaviors and feelings. Further, as Robin Leavitt points out in her powerful and disturbing book *Power and Emotion in Infant-Toddler Day Care*, there are times when, due to its unequal nature and to children's understandably limited ability to contribute to it, the caring relationship may not be enough to sustain even the most committed loving teacher's capacities for ongoing caregiving. This can lead to a great deal of emotional strain, anger, and alienation for the teacher. When teachers become burdened in this way, their loving feelings are transformed into "emotional labor—the publicly observable management of feelings sold for a wage" (1994, 61).

Leavitt's observations about the dark side of caring echo concerns raised by the feminists and early childhood educators discussed earlier in this book: some feminists, taking an anticaring stance, argue that putting women in a caring role traps them in a socially constructed image of femininity that is oppressive and limiting (Tronto 1989; Flax 1991); early childhood educators shy away from caring because it seems too soft, too unprofessional (Bloch 1987; Goldstein 1993). Both feminists and early childhood professionals conceive of caring as a step backward, into a more traditional and less powerful position, not a step forward toward more responsible and responsive decision making.

The bottom line question here is this: does love belong in school? As discussed in Chapter Four, Lisa Delpit's (1988) work on educating other people's children asserts that there are certain responsibilities accorded to the school and others accorded to the family. Perhaps love does not belong in school at all. Or perhaps it does. Perhaps it is just the word "love" that is problematic. It is slippery and unclear, used by everyone but defined by no one (Varenne 1977). Perhaps it has implicit or assumed sexual connotations that make it inappropriate for use in classroom contexts: relationship is a given, caring is fine, affection and fondness are acceptable, but love steps over the line. As Martha said in our dialogue journal: "It feels strange even to use the word love in writing or talking about students not because I don't feel love, but because I generally don't think it is expected and in some people's eyes acceptable and/or good to love students." Is it worth reclaiming the word "love," or should I be content to use a more acceptable term? If the term "love" puts people off, prevents them from seeing the value of centering teaching and learning around caring relationships, then perhaps "love" should be discarded. I am not as deeply committed to the term itself as I am to the way of being, the feelings, and the types of relationships and experiences that it denotes.

But watching Martha teaching her students suggests that there is more at work than a palatable, moderate term like "the ethic of care" would imply. As I have asserted in Chapter One, there is an element of passion, of fire, of joy to love that makes the ethic of care come to life in teaching with love. Martha's work with the children she teaches involves the interplay of passion, commitment, and intimacy that characterize love, as defined by Sternberg (1988a). Why avoid using a word that seems so appropriate? Nothing is lost in bringing love into the classroom, and I believe that there is much to be gained.

Because this study was a first attempt to examine the nature of love in classrooms, it raises more questions than it answers. There is much territory that still beckons, and many aspects of teaching with love that were not even touched upon in this research. Like an archaeologist, I can look out across the plain and wonder about the marvels that await, currently invisible but really just beneath the surface, in the ground all around my chosen excavation site. I can only begin to guess about the potential hidden in the terrain all around me.

But there are also questions that arise directly out of this research, questions that would require that I dig deeper into the issues I have begun to work with here. For example, I found Sternberg's triangular model of love to be useful for understanding love in classrooms, but it is not perfect. This leads to questions. What does Sternberg's model miss? What other conceptual frameworks could be used to explain and to understand the phenomenon of teacherly love? What would be gained by using other frameworks?

Looking at the work of more teachers who claim to root their teaching practices in love would be an important next step in developing the idea of loving teaching. Having a larger sample pool would enable me to grapple with the problematic questions of similarity and difference in philosophy and in practice raised by this study. It would also allow me to cast a wider net than I was able to in this study of two teachers, and I could explore the ways in which race, class, gender, educational background, ethnicity, religion, and professional training shape teachers' views on the acceptability and nature of emotion, caring, and relationships in the classroom. This would certainly enhance my understanding of the notion of teacherly love.

These types of questions raise more questions. In the middle class school district in which this study took place, two middle class teachers of white and Asian descent taught (with a handful of exceptions) 24 middle class children of white and Asian descent. There was a high level of cultural congruence between the teachers and our students. It would be interesting and important to look at the role of love in the teaching practices of professionals who teach children unlike themselves.

It would also be important to explore the impact of teaching with love on students. What is their experience of learning in a love-filled environment? What kind of difference does love make in their performance, in their learning, in their attitudes about school? Does it differ for boys and girls? Or for children of different races, classes, ethnicities? Do children in loving classroom environments tend to love their teachers more often than children in more traditional educational settings? What does it mean to have student-teacher relationships highlighted and acknowledged? Does teaching with love have an effect on children's self-esteem or self-concept? What is the nature of a child's love for a teacher? How does it relate and compare to the love children feel for their parents?

And what of students in other grade levels? It would be interesting to examine the role of love and the shape love takes in the upper elementary grades, in middle school, high school, and even college and graduate school. Is there a place for love in these classrooms?

Finally, I need to confront directly and to examine carefully the ambivalence that surrounds the word "love." One way to do so would be to look at the nature of teacherly love in the professional practices of teachers who do not explicitly teach with love as a guiding force in their work. Is it possible to be a loving teacher without knowing it? If so, what does that suggest about the utility of the concept of loving teaching? Further, it would be worthwhile to explore the boundaries between acceptable caring relationships with students and those tainted by "poisonous pedagogy": until this gray area is understood and clarified, the notion of love will remain highly charged, somewhat taboo, and marginalized in discussions of classroom life.

Given these complications, uncertainties, and unanswered questions, why would a teacher make the choice to teach with love? First of all, it benefits the children being taught. Teaching with love provides teachers with the opportunity to teach children more than academic knowledge and skills. Since, as Noddings (1984) points out, we learn how to care through the experience of being cared for, children taught with love will learn to be caring people. Teaching with love brings intimacy and the ethic of care into the classroom. It moves education a tremendous step ahead of what is possible through passion and commitment alone, a step that is, moreover, especially timely; as Martin's (1992) work on the schoolhome has indicated, children's needs both for care and for learning how to care are rapidly increasing in urgency. School is the logical place for these needs to be met.

A teacher might choose to teach with love out of his or her desire to enhance the emotional and personal lives of the students, or to enhance his or her own experiences in the classroom, both personal and professional. Teaching with love recognizes the emotional lives of teachers in their classrooms, after a long period during which teachers' feelings of attachment to their students have been dismissed or ignored (Henry 1963). As I have pointed out, even teachers who feel love are oftentimes unwilling to admit it. Choosing to teach with love legitimizes these feelings: it sets the record straight.

Further, loving teaching acknowledges that relationships with students are a significant source of professional satisfaction for teachers, what Lortie (1975, 104) calls the "psychic rewards" of teaching. Jennifer Nias (1989) found overwhelming evidence that teachers of young children felt that the opportunity to be deeply and personally involved with children was very satisfying and beneficial. One teacher highlighted the mutuality of the student-teacher relationship by saying, "Don't think I'm the one who's doing all the giving. . . . I know that by the end of the day several people will have shown that they love me" (Nias 1989, 87). Teaching with love allows teachers to use the benefits of classroom intimacy to balance out and to compensate for the intense levels of commitment and passion required to succeed in this demanding profession.

The decision to teach with love has the potential for impact beyond the classroom walls. If broadly adopted, loving teaching would have implications for teacher education, and for school reform. It is also possible to imagine reshaping educational policy, social policy, and even government legislation, around the notion of placing love for children at the center of our practice. Though these possibilities are beyond the scope of this book (see Martin 1992 or Edelman 1992 for discussions along these lines), teaching with love has implications, both for the field of early childhood education and for feminism as a discipline, which need to be considered here.

As I have pointed out earlier (see Chapter One), early childhood education is traditionally rooted in the field of developmental psychology. My discussion of developmentally appropriate practice and its critics suggests that although this heritage provides a great deal, there is much that is missing. Most notably absent from developmentally appropriate practice, for the purposes of this study, is attention to caring, interconnectedness, and mutual responsibility (Jipson 1991). If we drew upon feminist theory and ethics to flesh out our current vision of early childhood education we would greatly enhance what we are able to provide our children. Teaching with love blends perfectly with the reality of working with young children, as it builds on and further develops the early childhood educator's responsibility to care for young children.

In an effort to become "scientific and professional" (Bloch 1987) at the turn of the century, early childhood educators turned away from caring and love and embraced science as the primarily source of information about teaching the young. As I discussed in Chapter Five, recent developments in feminist thinkers have asserted that "scientific" and "professional" are problematic terms, terms that obscure some of the most important aspects of human interaction. Further, Clandinin's (1986) work on personal practical knowledge suggests that the love-based wisdom that early childhood educators possess as a result of lived experience with children (Smith 1987) is a legitimate and worthy knowledge, knowledge that needs to be taken seriously.

Perhaps it is time that early childhood education took a second look at love. "Scientific" knowledge should not stand alone as the sole foundation of our teaching practices. Teaching with love takes the emotional aspects of teaching young children, the caring and connection that characterize the best early childhood educational environments, and places them on an equal footing with more traditional, officially sanctioned sources of theoretical knowledge about children and child development. Loving teaching closes the gap between what we do with the young children in our care and how we feel about them. It gives legitimate intellectual authority to the affective heart of our profession.

One of the stated purposes of this study was to begin to develop a feminist vision of the education of young children. I proposed that teaching with love, a way of being in classrooms that operationalizes the feminist ethic of care, was one way to bring feminism and early childhood education together. As I have already discussed, rooting education in love has the potential to reshape the field of early childhood education. But what does loving teaching offer feminism?

Feminism, as it has evolved historically, is about women and women's experiences. Feminism is about women making themselves heard, claiming what is theirs, taking care of themselves. Feminism is not primarily about children. In fact, children can be seen as a wrench in the works of feminism. For example, both Charlotte Perkins Gilman and Henrietta Rodman, two of the early twentieth century's foremost feminist thinkers, were clearly ambivalent about the place of children in a woman's life: children seemed to be little more than a hindrance, a nuisance, a biological urge (Sochen 1972). These two thinkers looked out at the world and saw women trapped by their children, forced to remain in the private sphere, and thereby denied their rights as individuals, and thwarted in their attempts to grow as people. Though neither advocated childlessness as a feminist ideal, it was clear to them that it would make life easier. Contemporary writers on motherhood as an institution (Rich 1976; Firestone 1970; Allen 1982, among many others) have also grappled with these problems. Though many feminist thinkers are antimotherhood, none are explicitly antichild. But children are clearly problematic.

The relationship between feminism and young children is further complicated by the traditional association of women and children. Because women have long been linked with the low status occupations of child rearing and child care, many feminists have not rushed to associate themselves with the issues and concerns in these areas. Feminists have worked to free women from these stereotyped associations; it might be seen as counterproductive to turn our focus back to children.

As a result, feminisms have tended to focus firmly on adult experiences and concerns. When feminist theories are interpreted, translated, and applied to pedagogy, they retain their adult focus. Feminist education, rooted in the women's movement tradition of consciousness raising, is about adults educating themselves and other adults. Nothing inherent in feminist theory would prevent its pedagogical strategies or theoretical constructs from being used with children. But, as I have said, feminism is about women: children are simply not that high up on the feminist agenda. This would not be a problem were it not for feminism's transformative vision. Feminists, if it is possible to generalize about such a diverse group, aspire to improve the world, to make it a fairer, kinder, and more humane place for all people. Education, particularly of the young, plays a crucial role in social change. Feminist education cannot afford to ignore children, and teaching with love is one possible way of bringing children and feminism together.

The idea of teaching with love is not new or dramatically different. It has been at the heart of the educational experience all along, quietly enhancing teaching and learning relationships. It is a facet of the practices of many teachers, often surfacing in the form of teacherly love. But it is a facet that is usually ignored or dismissed as being unworthy for study because of the academic community's tendency to study phenomena that can be quantified and measured, things that are less "warm and fuzzy" than emotional relations. In this study I let love take center stage, and explored its character and parameters when allowed primacy in the classroom.

Putting love at the center of the educational enterprise enhances the experiences of both the children and the teachers involved. It has the potential to transform the field of early childhood education, giving intellectual authority to the emotional, interpersonal work that is at the heart of teaching young children. Teaching with love is also a way to bring young children under the umbrella of feminism, thus furthering its transformative agenda. We have nothing to lose by teaching with love. And we—and the children we teach—have everything to gain.

# References

Acker, J., Barry, K., and Esseveld, J. 1983. Objectivity and truth: problems in doing feminist research. *Women's Studies International Forum*, 6 (4): 423–35.

Acker, S. In press. Carry on caring: the work of women teachers. *British Journal of Sociology of Education*.

Ainsworth, M.D.S. 1978. *Patterns of attachment*. Hillsdale, NJ: Lawrence Erlbaum Associates.

Allen, J. 1982. Motherhood: the annihilation of women. In Treblicot, J. (ed.) 1984. *Mothering: essays in feminist theory*. Totowa, NJ: Rowman and Allanheld.

Aries, P. 1962. *Centuries of childhood: a social history of family life*. New York: Alfred A. Knopf.

Ashton-Warner, S. 1963. *Teacher*. New York: Touchstone Books.

Ayers, W. 1989. *The good preschool teacher*. New York: Teachers College Press.

Ayers, W. 1993. *To teach*. New York: Teachers College Press.

Badinter, E. 1980. *Mother love: myth and reality*. New York: Macmillan.

Ball, D.L. and Rundquist, S.S. 1993. Collaboration as context for joining teacher learning with learning about teaching. In Cohen, D.K., McLaughlin, M.W., and Talbert, J.E. (eds.), *Teaching for understanding*. San Francisco: Jossey-Bass.

Baumrind, D. 1986. Sex differences in moral reasoning: response to Walker's (1984) conclusion that there are none. In Larrabee, M.J. (ed.), 1993. *An ethic of care*. New York: Routledge.

Belenky, M.F., Clinchy, B.M., Goldberger, N.R., and Tarule, J.M. 1986. *Women's ways of knowing*. New York: Basic Books.

Bereiter, C. and Engelmann, S. 1966. *Teaching disadvantaged children in the preschool*. Englewood Cliffs, NJ: Prentice-Hall.

Bernard, J. 1975. *Women, wives and mothers: values and options*. Chicago: Aldine.

Bettelheim, B. 1987. *A good enough parent: A book on child-rearing*. New York: Knopf.

Biklen, S.K. 1992. Mothers gaze from teachers' eyes. In Biklen, S. and Pollard, D. (eds.), *Gender and education*. Chicago: National Society for the Study of Education.

Bloch, M.N. 1987. Becoming scientific and professional: an historical perspective on the aims and effects of early education. In Popkewitz, T.S. (ed.), *The formation of the school subjects*. New York: The Falmer Press.

Bloch, M.N. 1992. Critical perspectives on the historical relationship between child development and early childhood education research. In Kessler, S. and Swadener E.B. (eds.), *Reconceptualizing the early childhood curriculum*. New York: Teachers College Press.

Bloom, B. 1964. *Stability and change in human characteristics*. New York: Wiley.

Boulton, M.G. 1983. *On being a mother: a study of women with pre-school children*. New York: Tavistock Publications.

Bowlby, J. 1966. *Maternal care and mental health*. New York: Schocken Books.

Bowles, G. and Duelli Klein, R., eds. 1983. *Theories of women's studies.* London: Routledge and Kegan Paul.

Braithwaite, E.R. 1959. *To Sir, with love.* Englewood Cliffs, NJ: Prentice-Hall.

Brazelton, T.B. 1969. *Infants and mothers.* New York: Delacorte Press.

Bredekamp, S., ed. 1987. *Developmentally appropriate practice in early childhood programs serving children from birth through age 8.* Washington, D.C.: National Association for the Education of Young Children.

Bronfenbrenner, U. 1970. *Two worlds of childhood: U.S. and U.S.S.R.* New York: Sage Publications.

Bronfenbrenner, U. 1979. *The ecology of human development.* Cambridge, MA: Harvard University Press.

Brookes, A. and Kelly, U.A. 1989. Writing pedagogy: a dialogue of hope. *Journal of Education.* 171 (2): 117–31.

Bruner, J. 1960. *The process of education.* Cambridge, MA: Harvard University Press.

Bunch, C. and Pollack, S., eds. 1983. *Learning our way: essays in feminist education.* Trumansburg, NY: Crossing Press.

Burck, F.W., ed. 1986. *Mothers talking: sharing the secret.* New York: Saint Martin's Press.

California State Department of Education. 1987. *English-language arts framework for California public schools.* Sacramento, CA: California State Department of Education.

California State Department of Education. 1988. *Historysocial science framework for California public schools, kindergarten through grade 12*. Sacramento, CA: California State Department of Education.

Card, C. 1990. Caring and evil. *Hypatia*. 5 (1): 101–8.

Chapin, T. and Forster, J. 1988. Family tree. *Family Tree*. New York: Sundance Music.

Chodorow, N. 1978. *The reproduction of mothering: psychoanalysis and the sociology of gender*. Berkeley: University of California Press.

Clandinin, D.J. 1986. *Classroom practice*. London: The Falmer Press.

Clandinin, D.J. 1993. Learning to collaborate at the university: finding our places with each other. In Clandinin, D.J., Davies, A., Hogan, P., and Kennard, B. (eds.), *Learning to teach, teaching to learn*. New York: Teachers College Press.

Clandinin, D.J., Davies, A., Hogan, P., and Kennard, B., eds. 1993. *Learning to teach, teaching to learn*. New York: Teachers College Press.

Clarey, J., Hutchins, J., Powers, V., Thiem, L. 1985. Feminist education: transforming the research seminar. *Journal of Thought*. 20 (3): 147–61.

Collins, J. and Lazier, W. 1994. *Beyond entrepreneurship: turning your business into an enduring great company*. Englewood Cliffs, NJ: Prentice-Hall.

Collins, P.H. 1991. *Black feminist thought*. New York: Routledge.

Connelly, F.M. and Clandinin, D.J. 1990. Stories of experience and narrative inquiry. *Educational Researcher*. 19 (5): 2–14.

Conway, J.K. 1989. *The road from Coorain*. New York: Vintage Books.

Culley, M. and Portugues, C., eds. 1983. *Gendered subjects: the dynamics of feminist teaching*. Boston: Routledge and Kegan Paul.

Dally, A.G. 1982. *Inventing motherhood: the consequences of an ideal*. London: Burnett Books.

Darling, E. 1994. A tale of two schools. Ohlone: an open door. *Palo Alto Weekly*. 16(5): 20–4.

Davies, A. 1993. Learning planning without planning to learn. In Clandinin, D.J., Davies, A., Hogan, P., and Kennard, B. (eds.),. *Learning to teach, teaching to learn*. New York: Teachers College Press.

Delpit, L. 1988. The silenced dialogue: power and pedagogy in educating other people's children. *Harvard Educational Review*. 58 (3): 280–98.

Dewey, J. 1938. *Experience and education*. New York: Collier Books.

Dewey J. 1902/1990. *The school and society and The child and the curriculum*. Chicago: University of Chicago Press.

Dinnerstein, D. 1976. *The mermaid and the minotaur*. New York: Harper & Row.

Dixon, P. 1991. *Mothers and mothering: an annotated feminist bibliography*. New York: Garland Publishing.

Duelli Klein, R. 1983. How to do what we want to do. In Bowles, G. and Duelli Klein, R. (eds.), *Theories of women's studies*. London: Routledge and Kegan Paul.

Edelman, M.W. 1992. *The measure of our success*. Boston: Beacon Press.

Eisner, E. 1982. *Cognition and curriculum*. New York: Longman.

Eisner, E. 1985. *The educational imagination*. New York: Macmillan.

Eisner, E. 1991. *The enlightened eye*. New York: Macmillan.

Eliot, T.S. 1971. The hollow men. In *The complete poems and plays 1909–1950*. San Diego, CA: Harcourt, Brace, Jovanovich.

Elkind, D. 1981. *The hurried child*. Reading, MA: Addison-Wesley.

Elkind, D. 1989. Developmentally appropriate practice: philosophical and practical implications. *Phi Delta Kappan*. 71 (2): 113–7.

Escalante, J. 1990. The Jaime Escalante math program. *Journal of Negro Education*. 59 (30): 9.

Farganis, S. 1989. Feminism and the reconstruction of social science. In Jaggar, A.M. and Bordo, S.R. (eds.), *Gender/body/knowledge: feminist reconstructions of being and knowing*. New Brunswick, NJ: Rutgers University Press.

Firestone, S. 1970. *The dialectic of sex*. New York: Bantam Books.

Fisher, B. 1987. What is feminist pedagogy? *Radical Teacher*. 18: 20–4.

Flax, J. 1991. *Thinking fragments: psychoanalysis, feminism and postmodernism in the contemporary west*. Berkeley: University of California Press.

Florio, S. and Walsh, M. 1978. The teacher as colleague in classroom research. *Institute for Research on Teaching Occasional Paper No. 4*. East Lansing, MI: Michigan State University.

Florio, S. 1984. Very special natives: the evolving role of teachers as informants in educational ethnography. *Institute for Research on Teaching Occasional Paper No. 42*. East Lansing, MI: Michigan State University.

Florio-Ruane, S. 1986. Conversation and narrative in collaborative research. *Institute for Research on Teaching Occasional Paper No. 102.* East Lansing, MI: Michigan State University.

Fox, M. 1995. "Like mud not fireworks." The place of passion in the development of literacy. Paper presented at the symposium Teaching as an art, writing as a craft. The English-Language Arts Consortium of the Greater Bay Area, Redwood Shores, CA.

Fraiberg, S. 1977. *Every child's birthright: in defense of mothering.* New York: Basic Books.

Freedman, S. 1990. Weeding women out of "woman's true profession." In Antler J. and Biklen, S.K. (eds.), *Changing education.* Albany, NY: SUNY Press.

Freire, P. 1970. *Pedagogy of the oppressed.* New York: Seabury Press.

Freud, A. 1952. The role of the teacher. *Harvard Educational Review.* 22 (4): 229–43.

Fried, R.L. 1995. *The passionate teacher.* Boston: Beacon Press.

Friedan, B. 1963. *The feminine mystique.* New York: Dell.

Friedland, R. and Kort, C., eds. 1981. *The mothers' book: shared experiences.* Boston: Houghton Mifflin.

Gardner, H. 1983. *Frames of mind.* New York: Basic Books.

Gerber, M. 1979. *The RIE manual: for parents and professionals.* Los Angeles: Resources for Infant Educarers.

Gilligan, C. 1982. *In a different voice.* Cambridge, MA: Harvard University Press.

Gilligan, C. 1990. Teaching Shakespeare's sister: notes from the underground of female adolescence. In Gilligan, C., Lyons, N.P., and Hanmer, T.J. (eds.), *Making connections.* Cambridge, MA: Harvard University Press.

Glenn, E.N. 1994. Social construction of motherhood: a thematic overview. In Glenn, E.N., Chang, G., and Forcey, L.R. (eds.), *Mothering: ideology, experience, and agency.* New York: Routledge.

Glesne, C. and Peshkin, A. 1992. *Becoming qualitative researchers.* White Plains, NY: Longman.

Goldstein, L.S. 1993. The distance between feminism and early childhood education: an historical perspective. Paper presented at the conference Reconceptualizing Early Childhood Education: Theory, Research, and Practice, Ann Arbor, MI.

Goodlad, J.I. and Anderson, R.H. 1959. *The nongraded elementary school.* New York: Teachers College Press.

Greene, M. 1986. Reflection and passion in teaching. *Journal of Curriculum and Supervision.* 2 (1): 68–81.

Greeno, C.G. and Maccoby, E.E. 1986. How different is the "different voice"? *Signs : Journal of Women in Culture and Society* 11: 310–16.

Grieshaber, S. 1996. Beating mum: how to win the power game. Paper presented at the conference Reconceptualizing Early Childhood Education: Theory, Research, and Practice, Madison, WI.

Griffith, A.I. and Smith, D.E. 1987. Constructing cultural knowledge: mothering as discourse. In Gaskell, J.S. and McLaren, A.T. (eds.), *Women and education: A Canadian perspective.* Calgary, Alberta: Detselig Enterprises.

Grumet, M. 1988. *Bitter milk.* Amherst, MA: The University of Massachusetts Press.

Harding, S., ed. 1987. *Feminism and methodology: Social science issues.* Milton Keynes, England: Open University Press.

Hargreaves, A. 1994. *Changing teachers, changing times.* London: Cassell.

Harlow, H.F. 1986. *From learning to love.* New York: Praeger.

Heffner, E. 1978. *Mothering: the emotional experience of mothering after Freud and feminism.* New York: Doubleday.

Heilman, S.C. 1983. *The people of the book.* Chicago: University of Chicago Press.

Held, V. 1987. Feminism and moral theory. In Kittay, E.F. and Meyers, D.T. (eds.), *Women and moral theory.* New York: Rowman and Littlefield.

Helms, J. 1995. Personal conversation with author.

Henry, J. 1963. American schoolrooms: learning the nightmare. *Columbia University Forum.* 6: 24–30.

Hoagland, S.L. 1990. Some concerns about Nel Noddings' *Caring. Hypatia.* 5 (1): 109–14.

Hoberman, M.A. 1978. *A house is a house for me.* New York: Viking Press.

Hoffnung, M. 1989. Motherhood: contemporary conflict for women. In Freeman, J. (ed.), *Women: a feminist perspective.* Palo Alto, CA: Mayfield.

Hogan, P. 1993. Not finding the connections. In Clandinin, D.J., Davies, A., Hogan, P., and Kennard, B. (eds.), *Learning to teach, teaching to learn.* New York: Teachers College Press.

Holland, B. 1980. *Mother's Day: or, the view from in here.* Garden City, NY: Doubleday.

Houston, B. 1990. Caring and exploitation. *Hypatia.* 5 (1): 115–19.

Jackson, P.W. 1968/1990. *Life in classrooms.* New York: Teachers College Press.

Jaggar, A.M. 1989. Love and knowledge: emotion in feminist epistemology. In Jaggar, A. M. and Bordo, S.R. (eds.), *Gender/body/knowledge: feminist reconstructions of being and knowing.* New Brunswick, NJ: Rutgers University Press.

Jipson, J. 1991. Developmentally appropriate practice: culture, curriculum, connections. *Early Education and Development.* 2 (2): 120–36.

Kass, M. et al. 1993. *Ohlone School: 1993–94 report to the community.* Palo Alto, CA: Palo Alto Unified School District.

Katz, L.G. 1971. Sentimentality in preschool teachers: some possible interpretations. *Peabody Journal of Education.* 48 (2): 96–105.

Katz, L.G. 1981. Mothering and teaching: some significant distinctions. In *Ferguson Lectures in Education.* Evanston IL: National College of Education.

Kaufman, B. 1964. *Up the down staircase.* New York: Avon Books.

Kerber, L.K. 1986. Some cautionary words for historians. *Signs : Journal of Women in Culture and Society.* 11: 304–10.

Kessler, S. 1991a. Alternative perspectives on early childhood education. *Early Childhood Research Quarterly.* 6: 183–97.

Kessler, S. 1991b. Early childhood education as development: critique of the metaphor. *Early Education and Development.* 2 (2): 137–52.

Kessler, S. and Swadener, E. B., eds. 1992. *Reconceptualizing the early childhood curriculum.* New York: Teachers College Press.

Kidder, T. 1989. *Among schoolchildren.* New York: Avon Books.

Kittay E.F. and Meyers, D.T., eds. 1987. *Women and moral theory*. New York: Rowman and Littlefield.

Kitzinger, S. 1979. *Women as mothers: how they see themselves in different cultures*. New York: Random House.

Kleinmann, S. and Copp, M.A. 1993. *Emotions and fieldwork*. Newbury Park, CA: Sage Publications.

Kohl, H.R. 1967. *36 children*. New York: Signet Books.

Kohl, H.R. 1969. *The open classroom*. New York: Random House.

Kohl, H.R. 1984. *Growing minds*. New York: Harper & Row.

Kohlberg, L. 1981. *The philosophy of moral development*. San Francisco: Harper & Row.

Kohlberg, L. and Mayer, R. 1972. Development as the aim of education. *Harvard Educational Review*. 42 (4): 449–96.

Larrabee, M.J., ed. 1993. *An ethic of care*. New York: Routledge.

Lather, P. 1991. *Getting smart*. New York: Routledge.

Lazarre, J. 1986. *The mother knot*. Boston: McGraw-Hill.

Leavitt, R.L. 1994. *Power and emotion in infant-toddler day care*. Albany, NY: SUNY Press.

Levin, M. 1987. Parent-teacher collaboration. In Livingstone, D.W. (ed.), *Critical pedagogy and cultural power*. South Hadley, MA: Bergin and Garvey.

Lewis, C.S. 1953. *The abolition of man*. New York: Macmillan.

Lightfoot, S.L. 1977. Family-school interactions: the cultural image of mothers and teachers. *Signs: Journal of Women in Culture and Society*. 3 (2): 395–408.

Lightfoot, S.L. 1978. *Worlds apart: relationships between families and schools.* New York: Basic Books.

Lincoln, Y.S. and Guba, E.G. 1985. *Naturalistic inquiry.* Beverly Hills, CA: Sage Publications.

Lopate, P. 1975. *Being with children.* New York: Poseidon Press.

Lortie, D. 1975. *School teacher: a sociological study.* Chicago: University of Chicago Press.

Luria, Z. 1986. A methodological critique. *Signs: Journal of Women in Culture and Society* 11: 321–24.

Maher, F. 1983. Classroom pedagogy and the new scholarship on women. In Culley, M. and Portugues, C. (eds.), *Gendered subjects: the dynamics of feminist teaching.* Boston: Routledge and Kegan Paul.

Maher, F. 1987. Inquiry teaching and feminist pedagogy. *Social Education.* 51 (3): 186–92.

Malinowski, B. 1922. *Argonauts of the western Pacific.* London: Routledge.

Marshall, H. 1991. The social construction of motherhood: an analysis of childcare and parenting manuals. In Woollet, A., Phoenix, A. and Lloyd, E. (eds.), *Motherhood: meanings, practices, and ideologies.* London: Sage.

Martin, J.R. 1990. The contradiction of the educated woman. In Antler, J. and Biklen, S.K. (eds.), *Changing education.* Albany, NY: SUNY Press.

Martin, J.R. 1992. *The schoolhome.* Cambridge, MA: Harvard University Press.

Matthews, S.J. and Brinley, M.B. 1982. *Through the motherhood maze.* Garden City, NY: Doubleday.

McPherson, G.H. 1972. *Small town teacher.* Cambridge, MA: Harvard University Press.

Mead, M. 1961. *Coming of age in Samoa.* New York: Morrow.

Messer-Davidow, E. 1985. Knowers, knowing, knowledge: feminist theory and education. *Journal of Thought.* 20 (3): 8-24.

Metz, M.H. 1986. *Different by design.* New York: Routledge.

Mies, M. 1983. Towards a methodology for feminist research. In Bowles, G. and Duelli Klein, R. (eds.), *Theories of women's studies.* London: Routledge and Kegan Paul.

Mies, M. 1991. Women's research or feminist research. In Fonow, M.M. and Cook J.A. (eds.), *Beyond methodology: feminist scholarship as lived research.* Bloomington, IN: Indiana University Press.

Miller, A. 1983. *For your own good.* New York: Farrar, Straus, & Giroux.

Minturn, L. and Lambert, W.L. 1964. *Mothers of six cultures: antecedents of child-rearing.* New York: Wiley.

Narayan, U. 1989. The project of feminist epistemology: perspectives from a nonwestern feminist. In Jaggar, A.M. and Bordo, S.R. (eds.), *Gender/body/knowledge: feminist reconstructions of being and knowing.* New Brunswick, NJ: Rutgers University Press.

National Center for the Early Childhood Workforce. 1993. *Who cares?: childcare teachers and the quality of care in America.* Washington, D.C.: National Center for the Early Childhood Workforce.

National Education Association. 1993. *1993–1994 estimates of school statistics.* Washington, D.C.: National Education Association.

Nelson, M.K. 1994. Family day care providers: dilemmas of daily practice. In Glenn, E.N., Chang, G., and Forcey, L.R. (eds.), *Mothering: ideology, experience, and agency.* New York: Routledge.

Nettesheim, D.L. 1993. Moments in a year. In Clandinin, D.J., Davies, A., Hogan, P., and Kennard, B. (eds.), *Learning to teach, teaching to learn.* New York: Teachers College Press.

Nias, J. 1989. *Primary teachers talking.* London: Routledge.

Nicholson, L.J. 1983. Women, morality, and history. In Larrabee, M.J. (ed.), 1993. *An ethic of care.* New York: Routledge.

Noddings, N. 1984. *Caring.* Berkeley: University of California Press.

Noddings, N. 1992. *The challenge to care in schools.* New York: Teachers College Press.

Ohlone Elementary School. 1994. *The Ohlone code.* Palo Alto, CA: Palo Alto Unified School District.

Outka, G. 1972. *Agape.* New Haven, CT: Yale University Press.

Peshkin, A. 1986. *God's choice.* Chicago: University of Chicago Press.

Peters, R.S. 1959. Must an educator have an aim? In Peters, R.S. (ed.), *Authority, responsibility, and education.* London: Allen and Unwin.

Phoenix, A. and Woollet, A. 1991. Introduction. In Woollet, A., Phoenix, A. and Lloyd, E. (eds.), *Motherhood: meanings, practices, and ideologies.* London: Sage.

Polakow, V. 1993. *Lives on the edge.* Chicago: University of Chicago Press.

Powdermaker, H. 1966. *Stranger and friend.* New York: Norton.

Radl, S.L. 1973. *Mother's Day is over.* New York: Charterhouse.

Reinharz, S. 1983. Experiential analysis: a contribution to feminist research. In Bowles, G. and Duelli Klein, R. (eds.), *Theories of women's studies.* London: Routledge and Kegan Paul.

Reinharz, S. 1992. *Feminist methods in social research.* New York: Oxford University Press.

Ribbens, J. 1993. Standing by the school gate—the boundaries of maternal authority? In David, M., Edwards, R., Hughes, M. and Ribbens, J. (eds.), *Mothers and education: inside out?* New York: St. Martin's Press.

Rich, A. 1976. *Of woman born.* New York: Norton.

Richardson, V. 1994. Conducting research on practice. *Educational Researcher.* 23 (5): 5–10.

Rossiter, A. 1988. *From private to public: a feminist exploration of early mothering.* Toronto: The Women's Press.

Routman, R. 1988. *Transitions.* Portsmouth, NH: Heinemann.

Ruddick, S. 1987. Remarks on the sexual politics of reason. In Kittay E.F. and Meyers, D.T. (eds.), *Women and moral theory.* USA: Rowman and Littlefield.

Ruddick, S. 1989. *Maternal Thinking.* Boston: Beacon Press.

Sapon-Shevin, M. 1993. Comment made during session entitled Reconceptualizing theory and research in early childhood. American Educational Research Association, Atlanta, GA.

Schubert, W.H. and Ayers, W., eds. 1992. *Teacher lore.* White Plains, NY: Longman.

Singer, M.J. 1991. *Sound, image, and word in the curriculum: the making of historical sense.* Unpublished doctoral dissertation. Stanford University, Stanford, CA.

Smith, D.E. 1987. *The everyday world as problematic*. Boston: Northeastern University Press.

Sochen, J. 1972. *The new woman*. New York: Quadrangle Books.

Spodek, B. 1989a. Early childhood education in America: consistencies and contradictions. Paper presented at the International Conference on Early Education and Development, Hong Kong.

Spodek, B. 1989b. What should we teach kindergarten children? (Cassette Recording No. 612–89121). Alexandria, VA: Association for Supervision and Curriculum Development.

Stack, C.B. 1986. The culture of gender: women and men of color. *Signs : Journal of Women in Culture and Society*. 11: 321–24.

Stanley, L. and Wise, S. 1983. *Breaking out: feminist consciousness and feminist research*. London: Routledge and Kegan Paul.

Sternberg, R.J. 1988a. *The triangle of love*. New York: Basic Books.

Sternberg, R.J. 1988b. Triangulating love. In Sternberg, R.J. and Barnes, M.L. (eds.), *The psychology of love*. New Haven: Yale University Press.

Swadener, E.B. 1992. Comment made during discussion at conference Reconceptualizing Early Childhood Education: Theory, Research, and Practice. Chicago, IL.

Swigart, J. 1991. *The myth of the bad mother*. New York: Doubleday.

Thurer, S. L. 1994. *The myths of motherhood*. Boston: Houghton Mifflin.

Tronto, J.C. 1989. Women and caring: what can feminists learn about morality from caring? In Jaggar, A.M. and Bordo, E. (eds),

*Gender/body/knowledge: feminist reconstructions of being and knowing.* New Brunswick, NJ: Rutgers University Press.

Tronto, J.C. 1993. *Moral boundaries: A political argument for an ethic of care.* New York: Routledge.

Varenne, H. 1977. *Americans together.* New York: Teachers College Press.

Walker, A. 1983. *In search of our mothers' gardens.* New York: Harcourt Brace Jovanovich.

Walker, L.J. 1984. Sex differences in the development of moral reasoning: a critical review. In Larrabee, M.J. (ed.), 1993. *An ethic of care.* New York: Routledge.

Walsh, D.J. 1991. Extending the discourse on developmental appropriateness: a developmental perspective. *Early Education and Development.* 2 (2): 109–19.

Walsh, D.J. 1993. Time to move on: a few thoughts on a post-Piagetian/cultural psychology. Paper presented at the American Educational Research Association, Atlanta, GA.

Weiler, K. 1985. *Women teaching for change: gender, class, and power.* South Hadley, MA: Bergin and Garvey.

West, C. 1996. Democracy's promise, democracy's peril. *Association for Supervision and Curriculum Development Education Update.* 33 (3): 3.

Westkott, M. 1979. Feminist criticism of the social sciences. *Harvard Educational Review.* 49 (4): 422–30.

Whyte, W.F. 1943. *Street corner society.* Chicago: University of Chicago Press.

Wilson S.M. 1993. Deeply rooted change: a tale of learning to teach adventurously. In Cohen, D.K., McLaughlin, M.W., and

Talbert, J.E. (eds.), *Teaching for understanding*. San Francisco: Jossey-Bass.

Wolcott, H.F. 1990a. On seeking—and rejecting—validity in qualitative research. In Eisner, E.W. and Peshkin, A. (eds.), *Qualitative Inquiry in Education*. New York: Teachers College Press.

Wolcott, H.F. 1990b. *Writing up qualitative research*. Newbury Park, CA: Sage Publications.

# Index

Acker, A., 129, 131, 132
Acker, S., 120, 147, 151
Ainsworth, M.D.S., 18, 107
Allen, J., 105
Anderson, R.H., 39, 60
Aries, P., 107
Ashton-Warner, S., 151
Ayers, W. (Bill), 7, 34, 35, 151

Badinter, E., 107
Ball, D.L., 133, 134–5, 144
Barry, K., 129, 131, 132
Baumrind, D., 13
Belenky, M.F., 9
Bereiter, C., 25
Bernard, J., 106
Bettelheim, B., 116
Biklen, S.K., 110, 112, 160
Bloch, M.N., 4, 22, 27, 161, 165
Bloom, B., 23
Boulton, M.G., 106, 116
Bowlby, J., 18, 107
Braithwaite, E.R., 151
Brazelton, T.B., 116
Bredekamp, S., 3, 23, 25, 27, 51, 61,
    62, 110
Brinley, M.B., 116
Bronfenbrenner, U., 18
Brookes, A., 34
Bruner, J., 60
Burck, F.W., 106, 116

California State Department of
    Education, 89
Card, C., 15
Caring, 13–5, 26–7, 27–8, 29, 88
    contempt for, 115
    problems with, 15, 88–9, 161

Chang, G., 107
Chapin, T., 89
Chodorow, N., 105, 107
Clandinin, D.J., 75–6, 134, 139–40,
    141, 153, 156, 165
Clarey, J., 130
Clinchy, B.M., 9
Collaboration, 31–4, 89–91, 132–47
Collins, J., 73–4
Collins, P.H., 107
Commitment, 18, 19–20, 120–1,
    145–6, 152–3
Community, sense of, 78, 79–82, 93,
    143, 155
Connelly, F.M., 140
Copp, M.A., 33, 36

Dally, A.G., 106
Darling, E., 38
Davies, A., 76, 91
Delpit, L., 117–8, 161
Developmentally appropriate
    practice, 23–4, 61, 62, 165
Dewey, J., 22, 25, 29
Dinnerstein, D., 105, 107
Dixon, P., 105
Duelli Klein, R., 130, 131

Early childhood education
    definition of, 3–4
    feminism and, 4, 8–9, 24, 165–7
    history of, 22, 27, 165
    models of, 22–3
Edelman, M.W., 165
Eisner, E., 28, 31, 35, 50, 68, 69, 126
Eliot, T.S., 90
Elkind, D., 23, 110
Engelmann, S., 25

Escalante, J., 7
Esseveld, J., 129, 131, 132
Ethic of care, 1–2, 9–16, 129
　applied to schooling, 28–30

Farganis, S., 3, 9
Feminism
　children and, 166–8
　early childhood education and,
　　4, 8–9, 24, 165–7
　definitions of, 2–3
Feminist moral theory, 1, 11–6, 47,
　101–6
Feminist research methodologies,
　127, 128, 129–32
Feminist theory, 9–11
　applied to schooling, 28–30
Firestone, S., 105, 166
Fisher, B., 9, 10
Flax, J., 161
Florio (Ruane), S., 36, 128, 133, 136
Forcey, L.R., 107
Forster, J., 89
Fox, M., 16–7, 21, 24–5, 30, 149–51,
　158
Fraiberg, S., 105, 116
Freedman, S., 28
Freire, P., 131
Freud, A., 27, 118–9, 121, 149
Fried, R.L., 20–1
Friedan, B., 158
Friedland, R., 106

Gardner, H., 50
Gerber, M., 4
Gesell, A., 22
Gilligan, C., 11–3, 137, 142, 147
Gilman, C.P., 166
Glenn, E.N., 105, 107
Glesne, C., 68, 71, 76, 91, 125, 146
Goldberger, N.R., 9
Goldstein, L.S., 1, 22, 161
Goodlad, J.I., 39, 60
Greene, M., 17
Greeno, C.G., 13

Grieshaber, S., 108
Griffith, A.I., 117
Grumet, M., 1, 25, 97, 114, 115
Guba, E.G., 131

Harding, S., 130, 131
Hargreaves, A., 19, 119, 120, 121,
　151
Harlow, H.F., 18, 107
Heffner, E., 116
Heilman, S.C., 126, 128–9
Held, V., 13, 101–2, 153
Helms, J., 68
Henry, J., 149, 151, 154, 164
Hoagland, S.L., 15
Hoberman, M.A., 89
Hoffnung, M., 106
Hogan, P., 76, 140
Holland, B., 106
Houston, B., 15
Hutchins, J., 130

Intimacy, 18–9, 46, 80, 120, 145–6,
　159

Jackson, P.W., 7, 116
Jaggar, A.M., 28
Jipson, J., 24, 165

Katz, L.G., 26–7, 47, 93, 113, 118,
　119, 121, 160
Kaufman, B., 151
Kelly, U.A., 34
Kennard, B., 76
Kerber, L.K., 13
Kessler, S., 4, 22, 23, 24
Kidder, T., 70, 97, 151
Kittay, E.F., 11
Kitzinger, S., 107
Kleinmann, S., 33, 36
Kohl, H.R., 72–3, 79, 150–1, 158
Kohlberg, L., 11–2, 22
Kort, C., 106

Lambert, W.L., 106, 107
Lather, P., 128, 131
Lazarre, J., 106
Lazier, W., 73
Leavitt, R.L., 161
Levin, M., 112
Lewis, C.S., 20
Lightfoot, S.L., 109, 110, 112, 115,
    116, 119, 121, 149, 160
Lincoln, Y.S., 131
Lopate, P., 151
Lortie, D., 19, 93, 164
Love
    definition of, 17
    Lisa's thoughts on, 70–1, 72, 83
    Martha's thoughts on, 47–8,
        113–4
    triangular model, 18–21, 145–6
Luria, Z., 13

Maccoby, E.E., 13
Maher, F., 10, 130, 131
Malinowski, B., 126
Marshall, H., 108
Martin, J.R., 1, 16, 28–9, 30, 120, 165
Maternal thinking, 25, 47, 103–4
Matthews, S.J., 116
Mayer, R., 22
McPherson, G.H., 112, 119
Mead, M., 126
Messer–Davidow, E., 131
Metz, M.H., 126
Meyers, D.T., 11
Mies, M., 3, 9, 131
Miller, A., 79, 82–3, 85, 161
Minturn, L., 106, 107
Montessori, M., 28
Moral theory, 11–2
Motherhood
    conflict between teachers and
        mothers, 111–2, 114–7
    feminist writings on, 101–6,
        114–6
    while teaching, 25–7, 96–8, 110

Motherly love, 97–8, 106–10
    compared to teacherly love,
        113–4, 118–21
Multi-age classrooms, 38, 39–40, 48,
    51, 60–1

Narayan, U., 3, 9
National Association for the
    Education of Young Children,
    The (NAEYC), 23, 25, 51, 62, 110
National Center for the Early
    Childhood Workforce, The, 7
National Education Association,
    The, 7
Neill, A.S., 22
Nelson, M.K., 120
Nettesheim, D.L., 91
Nias, J., 19, 119, 151, 164–5
Nicholson, L.J., 13
Noddings, N., 13–5, 25, 29–30, 63,
    88, 104, 120, 125, 129, 153, 164

Outka, G., 152

Parents, 24–5
    response to Martha's teaching,
        111–2
Passion, 18, 20–1, 121, 145–6, 149
Personal practical knowledge 75–6,
    153, 165–6
Peshkin, A., 68, 71, 76, 91, 124, 125,
    146
Peters, R.S., 127
Phoenix, A., 108
Piaget, J., 22
Poisonous pedagogy, 79, 82–3, 85–
    6, 161
Polakow, V., 107
Powdermaker, H., 137
Powers, V., 130
Professional authenticity, feelings
    of, 67–8, 91–5, 99

Radl, S.L., 116
Reinharz, S., 127, 130, 131, 132

Teachers commonly talk about loving their students, yet no effort has been made to explore the powerful educational potential inherent in these loving feelings. *Teaching with Love* breaks new ground by paying careful, scholarly attention to the nature, the scope, the dimensions, and the variety of teacherly love. In a highly readable narrative that builds on the feminist notion of an ethic of care and draws from the fields of psychology and women's studies, this book examines and analyzes the experiences of two primary grade teachers as they set about trying to create and enact a vision of early childhood education centered around loving relationships.

"This beautifully written book is not afraid to speak of love in connection with teaching. It speaks also of the delicate nature of professional interactions and healthy differences in the ways good teachers approach teaching. Bold and stimulating."

*Nel Noddings*
*Lee L. Jacks Professor of Child Education*
*School of Education, Stanford University*

**Lisa S. Goldstein** is an assistant professor of Curriculum and Instruction at the University of Texas at Austin, where she teaches in the Early Childhood Education and the Curriculum Studies programs. She received her Ph.D. in Education from Stanford University, and is a former primary grade teacher.

PETER LANG PUBLISHING